MARIN SORESCU was born in the
of Dolj, the fifth child of a
attended secondary schools in Craiova and Predeal,
graduating from Iaşi University in Philology. Since 1978
he has been working as editor-in-chief of the literary
review *Ramuri*.

His first volume of poetry *Singur Printre Poeţi* (Alone
Amongst Poets) appeared in 1964, followed by numerous
volumes of poetry, prose and drama.

His first play, *Jonah*, was published in 1968, followed
by *The Verger* in 1970, and *The Matrix* in 1973. In 1974
the three were included as a trilogy in *The Thirst of the
Salt Mountain*. This trilogy has been translated by
Andrea Deletant and Brenda Walker and was published
by Forest Books in 1985. *Vlad Dracula the Impaler* was
written in 1978 and is set in mid-15th century Wallachia,
the original title being *The Impaler's Third Stake*.

His work has been translated into many languages, and
his plays performed throughout the world.

In 1974 he was awarded the prize for drama by the
Writers' Union of Romania and in 1978 the international
prize 'Le Muze' by the Academia delle Muze, Florence.
In 1983 he was made a correspondent member of the
Mallarmé Academy in Paris and in December of the
same year he received the International Poetry Prize
'Fernando Riello' in Madrid.

DENNIS DELETANT is lecturer in Romanian language and
literature at the School of Slavonic and East European
Studies, University of London. His publications include
Colloquial Romanian (Routledge & Kegan Paul, 1983)
and *Romania: World Bibliographical Series. Volume 59*
(Clio Press, 1985).

MARIN SORESCU

VLAD
DRACULA
THE IMPALER

The Lubeck portrait of Dracula published in Nuremberg in 1488.

VLAD
DRACULA
THE IMPALER

A PLAY
by
MARIN SORESCU

translated
by
DENNIS DELETANT

FOREST BOOKS
LONDON   ☆   1987   ☆   BOSTON

Published by FOREST BOOKS
20 Forest View, Chingford, London E4 7AY, U.K.
61 Lincoln Road, Wayland, MA. 01788, U.S.A.

First published 1987
Reprinted 1990

Typeset in Great Britain by Cover to Cover, Cambridge
Printed in Great Britain by A. Wheaton & Co Ltd, Exeter

Jacket design © Ann Evans
Translation © Dennis Deletant

British Library Cataloguing in Publication Data:
Sorescu, Marin
Vlad Dracula the Impaler
1. Sorescu, Marin
ISBN 0–948259–98–1

Library of Congress Catalog Card Number
86–082941

Contents

Photographs from the performance at The National Theatre at Cluj in Romania, directed by Mircea Marin.

We should like to thank the School of Slavonic & East European Studies, University of London, for its support in the publication of this translation.

Preface

For a dramatist, history is like a bone to a dog. It arouses that state of covetous exaltation, the eyes grow larger at such a heap of facts and ready-made dramas, all senses are alerted. Inspiration wets the lips and wags its tail; the marrow of life stands before it – enticing it.

I wrote *The Third Stake* several years ago and then had in mind various stage presentations and certain intonations of actors, but I can no longer remember them. On the eve of the publication of this English translation, I have re-read the text 'with new and different eyes' as the saying goes. In essence, the problem posed here is one of symmetry, but how far is it resolved? This is a personal opinion, but the moments of leaping backwards and forwards occur only when this symmetry is lost, when imbalance occurs. The Roman poet Lucretius spoke of atoms which deviate, which fall awkwardly in the void, and thought that from this small deviation life was created – an aberration, a happening in the cosmos. I have tried to study, both as poet and playwright, several of these knots of world history which, when unravelled, have had repercussions on Romanian history as well – on my personal history, to coin a phrase. Such a knot is the fall of Byzantium.

After the fall of Byzantium the great Sultan Mohammed II advanced further with the map of Europe in his hand, and, crossing the Danube, wanted to capture a citadel which was not marked on the map, to conquer a people small in number led by an unknown ruler, Vlad the Impaler. The campaign had no clear outcome. In essence it was a defeat, of symbolic significance. Of course it wasn't the military campaign that interested me – this being a matter for specialists – but everything behind it, in the 'folds of the facts'. The chain of symmetries and assymetries.

On stage there are two stakes, where two thieves are impaled, who, on symmetrically opposite grounds, have received the same punishment. Vlad, who has in mind to outdo the Sultan in cruelty, comes and takes lunch in front of the dying men and consults them, their death throes raising his morale, and he gives the order for a third stake to be placed between them which will remain unoccupied until he catches the chief villain. And who is this to be? We don't know. This empty stake destroys symmetry and creates the tension of further unravelling of the knot. Then there are the two leaders who face each other, one coming with a huge well-organized army, and the prestige of a military genius who has caused a great empire to fall, the other at the head of a handful of fighting men, more peasants and townsmen than soldiers, who succeeds in provoking confusion, fear, and finally, for just an instant, in removing the threat. Vlad will sacrifice himself, trapped as he is in this implacable mechanism of events and his own character, anxious to bring absolute justice 'down to the last subject', which happens to be none other than himself. The principal hero is, however, the common folk, who create through tens of individual destinies a great river of tragedy. A little medieval Romanian history does not go amiss amid so much world history, especially as the events have the value of an emblem, and, through translation, can be placed anywhere, and in any time, forwards or backwards. In their heart of hearts, at their spiritual core, people are the same everywhere, they have the same thoughts, the same aspirations. They get by as best they can and react identically in identical situations.

The Third Stake is a play about a certain situation, about a state of conflict. 'I don't like the times', says a rather eccentric character, who allows himself to escape from the present in search of better times. Vlad cannot escape and tries, in his desperate way to better the times in which he lives. I have tried to see him rather differently, more in keeping with the historical truth, with an astonishment but also with an understanding that tragic destinies always awake in us. From this point of view the play can also have a polemical character, casting another light on the famous legend.

I shan't be long-winded, because a preface, generally speaking, mustn't be longer than the work it introduces. I feel like giving up writing plays and prefaces when I think that Shakespeare would have written this in the form of a verse prologue, and Lord, with what artistry, and with how many plays upon words between 'history' and 'anecdote', and with what masterly definitions of history! Anyway this one is almost finished. I'll go back to the beginning: It is generally said of writers that they have, or lack, a good intuition of the present. I have tried to practise my intuition of the past. An exercise in shooting with a bow and arrow. An exercise in moving the moving targets at which you release your arrow. A supplement to the ebb of time which has long drifted down the hour-glass.

It so happens that as I write these words it's snowing outside. I look out of the window and see that the flakes are slipping obliquely from the sky towards the roof-tops to the ground. Like the atoms of Lucretius. The theory of assymetry is proved yet again. Now let's see the play.

Marin Sorescu

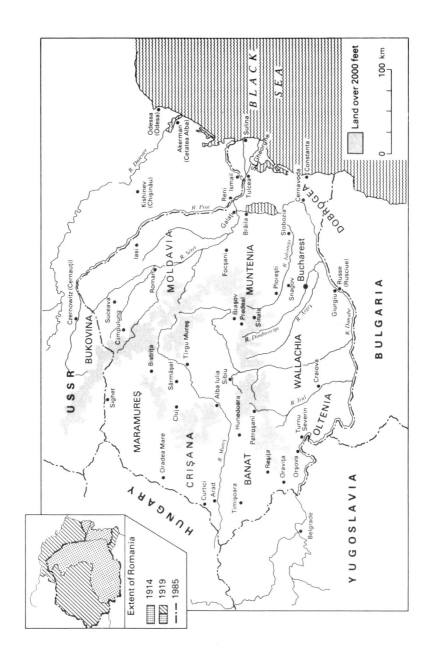

Introduction

The only connection between Vlad Dracula the Impaler, Prince of the Romanian principality of Wallachia, and Bram Stoker's Dracula is in the choice of the novel's name. Nothing in Stoker's fictional work bears a historical relationship to the deeds of Vlad or to the events of his reign. Vlad did not practise vampirism, nor is there any association of it with him in Romanian folk legend. Admittedly, the notoriety surrounding Vlad Dracula's method of punishment for his enemies, namely impalement, and other acts of cruelty attributed to him, provided Stoker with an attractive pedigree for his hero. But there the relationship ends.

By contrast, Marin Sorescu's drama *A treia ţeapa* (The Third Stake) has a strong factual basis. The historical Dracula, Vlad the Impaler, emerges from it as a victim of his time, an almost tragic figure who was in turn abandoned and imprisoned by his relative through marriage, Matthew Corvin, King of Hungary (1458–1490), betrayed by his brother Radu, and finally murdered by the Turks with the collusion of the Wallachian boyars at the close of 1476. The turbulence of the age is reflected in the fact that Vlad was ruling prince on three separate occasions: autumn 1448, 1456–1462, and November to December 1476; and that during the intervening periods he was held hostage by the Turks (1442–1448), was a fugitive in neighbouring Moldavia and Transylvania (1448–1456), and was imprisoned at Buda (1462–1474).

Wallachia during the fifteenth century was in the front line of Christian Europe's defence against the Ottoman Turks. When Constantinople, the bulwark of Christendom against the infidel, collapsed in 1453, the kingdoms of Hungary and Poland and their client states assumed the defence of western civilization against the threat from the south-east. The Romanian principalities of Moldavia and Wallachia were thrust into the crucible of confrontation between Christian and Muslim, between West and East, and in the process their very existence was threatened. As Christian princes the rulers of both principalities recognized that their fate was bound to that of their more powerful Christian neighbours to the north and west. Both Vlad the Impaler and Stephen the Great campaigned against the Turks, the latter winning the accolade of 'athlete of Christ' from the Pope; Vlad received the praise of the Byzantine chronicler Laonik Khalkokondiles who hailed him in 1463 as 'a hero of Christianity' for his defeat of the Sultan Mohammed II on the Danube. Nevertheless, neither Romanian prince was prepared to sacrifice his limited autonomy to the territorial ambitions of the monarchs of Poland and Hungary. A 'modus vivendi' between the Turks on the one hand, and the Poles and Hungarians on the other, became the principal preoccupation of the Romanian princes.

The achievement of this required a period of internal stability, the consolidation of central authority, and the organisation of an effective army. All three were pursued by Vlad, just as they were by his more illustrious contemporary in Moldavia, Stephen the Great. The methods employed by Vlad were no more drastic than those of Stephen, or of the Sultan Mohammed II or of Louis XI of France. Indeed the play itself recognises this: 'I was cruel in inflicting pain,' says Vlad, 'but the age was one of terror.' This is not to claim that the notoriety surrounding Vlad's name throughout Central and Eastern Europe in the latter part of the fifteenth century is completely undeserved. Yet there is good reason to believe that many of the acts of horrific cruelty attributed to him are spurious. The basis for such accusations are German pamphlets printed in Nuremburg and Augsburg between 1488 and 1530. The story of Dracula, as Vlad became known in the Latinized form of his name (from Vlad Dracul in Romanian, meaning Vlad the Dragon, so-called because he bore a cross with a dragon on his escutcheon), was published in several editions in German in the 1490s and many sensational details are believed to have been provided by the Saxon merchants of Transylvania, incensed by Vlad's suppression of their trading privileges in Wallachia.

The particular form of punishment with which Vlad is identified is impalement. Sorescu's play opens on such a scene, yet the play is not about Vlad's cruelty. It uses the events of his career as an allegory for the fear and fatalism that characterises the Romanians. There is no suggestion here of Bram Stoker's un-dead vampire Dracula or of a quest to conquer eternity – features of the Dracula legend which explain its continued popular appeal. Sorescu's Vlad is a prisoner of his own predicament, condemned to sacrifice himself on the third stake for the suffering of an ill-starred people. Vlad's misfortune is to believe that he can extirpate deceit, greed and theft, seen as concomitants of Wallachia's geographical position. The parallel with the country's twentieth century predicament is obvious to anyone familiar with Romania's present situation, and particularly to the Romanian theatre-goer. If you have ever visited contemporary Romania you may well appreciate even more the irony of many of Vlad's utterances and actions, some of which give the listener a feeling of *déjà entendu*. For instance, the conversation between Dan and Tenea about plans to move the capital from Tîrgovişte to Bucharest earn Sorescu the right to be considered a soothsayer; Vlad built a small palace for himself at Bucharest in 1459. A return to Tîrgovişte is but one indication that as a model for Romanian rulers Vlad is as important as Machiavelli.

A sense of fear and uncertainty pervades the play. Once again the present comes to mind. The contemporary poet Mircea Dinescu speaks of the Romanians' 'great provisions of tolerance and fear'. Vlad's actions are cruel, yet they find support from his very victims. The impaled Turk in the opening scene opines: 'Mohammed will go down in history as the tyrant of all tyrants. A great man! And that's why I think Vlad's got it right.' Such tolerance is another hallmark of the Romanian character.

Marin Sorescu's drama is a masterly encapsulation of the Romanian historical predicament. That artists of his stature have emerged in contemporary Romanian society is a testimony to that predicament.

Characters

VLAD DRACULA, called the Impaler, reigning prince of Wallachia
PAPUC, army commander
TENEA, a boyar, court counsellor
DRAGAVEI, a townsman
DAN, pretender to the throne
GĂGĂUȚA, Tenea's henchman
THE ROMANIAN, a Romanian
THE TURK, a Turk
DOMNICA, a princess living at the court of the Impaler
THE PAINTER, an Italian painter
JOIȚA, a pauper
SAFTA, a commoner
MINICA, a visionary
CHIORU and PÎRVU, executioners
AGA CARASOL and SULEIMAN, Turks who have come to collect
    the tribute
MARIȚA, Domnica's servant
THE CAPTAIN
A CRIPPLE
A crowd of paupers, commoners, soldiers.

The action takes place in Wallachia, about the middle of the 15th
century.

16

ACT
ONE

Morning

Hie facht fich an gar ein grauſſem

liche erſchröckenliche hyſtorien. von dem wilden wü-
trich Dracole weyde Wie er die leüt geſpiſt hat vnd
gepraten vñ mit den haübtern yn einē keſſel geſotten

Scene 1

Darkness. The figures of two men can be dimly seen. Silence, then the following dialogue is heard through the darkness.

'I'm afraid you're wrong about the cloud. It's got nothing to do with your rheumatism.'

'All right then, what other reason can you give for this agonising pain? Listen . . . it's like this: mist rising from the ground forms a ball. The ball gets bigger and as it does so absorbs the vapour on your spine. Then . . . '

'No, no, no! That's got nothing to do with it! I'll tell you why it hurts.'

'[*Curious*] All right then, why?

'Guess!'

'Why?'

'It hurts because you're not going to win the war.'

'What! You mean to say that my bones ache just because of Mohammed?'

'That's right.'

'Ache, my arse! Now you listen, I'm not on his side just because I believe in him, you know.'

'I know, I know.'

'And I'm not afraid of him . . . well, now I come to think of it, I am afraid . . . Have you ever felt fear? That's how we were brought up you know.'

'How?'

'In fear. It's something dim and you're never sure where it's coming from – like damp.'

'We're the same.'

'No, you're not afraid; or if you are now, you weren't before you grew up.'

19

'That's worse!'

'No, it isn't. When you're a child, a normal life and one of terror are two very different things. We never felt the serenity of childhood – that kind of safe wall – and when things got difficult, we had nothing to lean on.'

'You should have leant on that cloud.'

'All right, all right! Anyway that's why I believe Mohammed is a great . . . '

'Tyrant and a butcher.'

'Well, if he is, he's certainly an extraordinary one! I mean just think how he's spiritually maimed a whole universe. It's very easy to chop off a head – for instance mine's been chopped off already – but to force yourself into the soul of half the world and change their way of thinking – now that's really something.'

'In other words – to make them stop thinking.'

'To ruin the mechanism of thought. And that's why you, you who are free people . . . [*Bitterly*] I don't suppose you can understand us. [*Admiringly*] Ah, Mohammed will go down in history as the tyrant of all tyrants. A great man! And that's why I think Vlad's got it right . . . '

'No, you listen to me. He's wrong as well.'

[*Annoyed*] 'Then how can one stop a wave of crime? By just sitting on your arse all day doing nothing?'

[*Laughing*] 'I'd like to catch Prince Vlad doing that!'

[*Admiringly*] 'I tell you, Vlad outshines Mohammed.'

The stage is now lit and the two men become visible: A TURK *and a* ROMANIAN *are each impaled upon a stake. There is a brief silence.*

ROMANIAN: Day's breaking.

TURK: It'll be us who'll be breaking soon. Both of us. [*Looking into the distance*] You know there's something familiar about all this. It wouldn't surprise me to find that this is the place where I originally came from. Here.

ROMANIAN: [*Deliberately*] Did you return just to see your native country once again?

TURK: Longing for one's country makes you pine away. [*Still looking into the distance*] What's that, over there?

ROMANIAN: [*Looking in the opposite direction as he is unable to turn his head*] What?

TURK: Look straight ahead.

ROMANIAN: I am but I can only see forest.

TURK: I can see forest on this side too, but is there anyone in it?

ROMANIAN: Only the two of us. But it won't be long before the others get a turn.

TURK: Then that means you're strong and will take a long time to die.

ROMANIAN: You're beginning to get on my nerves. It's all right for you to keep on getting at us, you who took yourself off when you were young. It's all a pack of lies! Why can't you try seeing our good points for a change?

TURK: They've set you a bit higher than me. You've got a better vantage point. What are these good points you keep talking about? I wouldn't mind seeing them for myself!

ROMANIAN: Oh it's very easy for a man turned Turk to say bad things about his own country. You've no idea how difficult it's been for us to manage – the sacrifices that poor Prince has had to make just to save face. For more than a century we've been sucked dry by this Turkish leech. [*Spitefully*] While you lot have reduced us to nothing more than beggars.

TURK: Turks . . . or Tartars . . . Where's the difference?

ROMANIAN: That's the problem . . . they all swoop down on us like vultures or crows.

TURK: [*Scared*] What, have the crows come then? That means we're near the end.

ROMANIAN That's life!

TURK: I'll tell you something. I didn't *turn* Turk like you said. I was snatched from my mother's breast when barely twelve months old and given away as part of the tribute. Now that's not the same as turning Turk. I tell you, I loathe this ramshackle affair called Moslem power.

ROMANIAN: [*Thinking aloud*] He's coming, no he's not, yes he is, no he's not . . .

TURK: Who's coming?

ROMANIAN: He should've been here by now. He usually likes his breakfast near his victims, has a chat with them, gets a few things off his chest, asks their advice, and drinks their health. But he's got a sharp tongue in his head. Them that are impaled can't stomach him because of his lashing tongue.

TURK: [*Trying hard to laugh*] Ha!

The stage grows dark

21

ROMANIAN: [*Cheerfully*] Look it's hiding behind the clouds, the old fool . . .

TURK: It's going to get worse . . .

ROMANIAN: Well at least you can't see what's hurting you or how . . .

A pause

TURK: Why did you decide to cross the enemy lines?

ROMANIAN: Curiosity! [*Pauses*] I'd heard you'd solved some of your problems best you could. [*Laughing*] Tell me how does it feel to marry five women at the same time?

TURK: No different.

ROMANIAN: Go on, you're having me on!

TURK: Well, there is ONE difference. You've got five nags instead of one giving you hell!

ROMANIAN: Still! [*Changing the subject*] You might've known they'd catch you.

TURK: I thought there'd be plenty of time to explain . . . I was afraid of my own people . . . and of drowning in the Danube . . . I'd been trying to learn to swim for the last five years . . . practised in the dust . . .

ROMANIAN: [*Wickedly*] And the moment you got to the other side they got you!

TURK: That's about it. I mean I didn't even try to steer clear of them. I kept saying to myself: I'll explain that the Turks took me when I was very young . . .

ROMANIAN: [*Groaning*] Oooooh!

TURK: [*Continuing*] . . . and God wanted me to come back to see the house where I was born. I *didn't* avoid them and that's exactly what I said. If only I'd kept out of sight . . .

ROMANIAN: I did . . . and when I jumped in the water, there was a noose round my neck.

TURK: Well, things can usually go either way.

ROMANIAN: [*Reasoning*] I wasn't going to stay with the Turks. Oh, no. Not me. I thought I'd just have a good look round, see what was going on and then come back . . . full of it.

TURK: God, how it hurts . . .

ROMANIAN: I felt better in the light

The scene is lit again

ROMANIAN: Can you see any cloud on your side of the sky?
TURK: There's another on its way.

A pause

ROMANIAN: The ravens will be here by nightfall. Are you afraid of them?
TURK: Well, I've never been raven-sick.
ROMANIAN: They go for the eyes first . . .
TURK: They're almost plucked out already. Man suffers all his life.
TURK: Really?
ROMANIAN: In our country there used to be . . . I mean in their country, Turkey, there was a man who while still a child started to cut off pieces of his own skin. 'Let's suffer a bit today,' he'd say and off came a bit of flesh! In fact, because he feared death, he thought he'd get used to pain a bit at a time . . . so that at that moment when he'd suffer most . . . do you follow me . . . ?
ROMANIAN: Of course. He was no fool! But nowadays . . .
TURK: He WAS a fool! He'd almost reached his neck when he was denounced by someone or other because he was supposed to have said something. He did moan . . .
ROMANIAN: Daily?
TURK: Yes.
ROMANIAN: He was brave.
TURK: And when they got round to chopping off his head, they did it rather slowly so that he kept screaming out at the top of his voice that the pain was nothing in comparison to what he'd suffered already. Never before had he experienced such torture. All that training for nothing.
ROMANIAN: Well, after all, death is death. Hm! [*The Turk groans and then there is a long silence*] Did you say something? [*Silence*] Listen, Turk. Don't go and die before me or there'll be nobody left to talk to. [*Silence*] The Prince isn't coming after all.
TURK: What?
ROMANIAN: I thought that . . . Now don't you go and die on me too soon . . . Let's wait and see what happens.
TURK: I don't care any more.
ROMANIAN: Well, pretend to.
TURK: I couldn't care less . . . but I'd like to live a bit longer . . . Just now I thought I was going to faint.
ROMANIAN: [*Scared*] If I go all quiet keep talking to me.

TURK: I promise.
ROMANIAN: I shouldn't like to fall asleep. In this condition . . .
You never know what I might dream . . . I'm afraid . . .
TURK: At any rate, you can't fall out of bed. So if you groan, it
means you can't feel pain anymore and you're not asleep.
ROMANIAN: [*As an idea flashes across his mind*] Let's see who can
groan the longest.
TURK: All right.
ROMANIAN: Let's start together . . .
TURK: Right. Ready? One, two, three . . . [*They start howling in
unison*] Allah, Allah, Allah . . . !
ROMANIAN: [*Groaning*] Oh God, God, God . . . !

Scene 2

*Prince Vlad Dracula the Impaler makes his appearance, goes over to the
stakes, checks to see if they are firm in the ground and then stares at the
two men.*

VLAD: *[Rubbing his hands*] Well done! [*Sits on a stump*] I'm starving.
[*Claps his hands*]

DOMNICA *appears*

DOMNICA: Your pleasure, my Lord?
VLAD: I'm starving.

DOMNICA *goes out*

ROMANIAN: [*In a low voice to the Turk*] He's that greedy. It won't
be long before he starts chewing, sucking and smacking his lips.
I can't stand anyone eating right under my nose. It'll make me
hungry just for a chunk of bread or some meat. This rotten belly
of mine's as greedy as a pregnant woman.
TURK: Shut up, and be patient – 'til you're . . . delivered!
DOMNICA: [*Enters with a roast chicken and a loaf of bread. She lays it
on a cloth before the Prince*] Roast chicken, your Highness.
ROMANIAN: [*In a low voice*] My mouth's watering. Roast chicken!
DOMNICA: Do you want your supper out here this evening?

VLAD: Yes, in this fine company here. [*Pointing to the two men*]

DOMNICA: [*Pitifully*] Poor wretches. Your Highness. [*She exits*]

For a few moments Vlad stuffs down his food hurriedly. Silence. The Romanian sighs.

TURK: He doesn't say much.

VLAD: [*Having appeased his hunger a little, he turns to look at the stakes. Laughing*] So you'd like to die, but can't make the effort, eh? [*Sniffing*] God, you stink! You no sooner got into lofty positions than you start stinking. It's a strange thing that man always makes the place he lives in stink to high heaven. How old are you, lad?

ROMANIAN: Twenty.

VLAD: Gone twenty?

ROMANIAN: Gone, Your Highness. Gone for good and all . . . by Your Highness's pleasure.

VLAD: Fine. Fine!

TURK: On the contrary, that's very bad! I've never seen a braver man than this one here. You're going to miss him, you know.

VLAD: [*To the Romanian*] You're green. That's why you talk like that. In fact when you're twenty . . .

ROMANIAN: [*Laughing*] Did you say 'green', Your Highness? Not long ago the Turk here was telling me that we'd ripen in the sun.

VLAD: You won't be so talkative when you're old enough to understand.

ROMANIAN: Are you old enough, Your Highness?

VLAD: Yes.

ROMANIAN: Too bad!

VLAD: I'll ignore that! I haven't achieved all that much. Do you think it's easy getting a country on its feet again? [*Claps his hands. Domnica appears*] Can't you even get a glass of wine around here? I want to drink the health of these two men.

Scene 3

DOMNICA: That's highly unlikely, Your Highness! Oh, I keep forgetting you told me to call you uncle. We've plenty of wine

25

but no glasses. When the Turks were last here, they played havoc with everything. You know how they are; breaking and wrecking things. Whenever they pass through here everything's smashed to pieces.

VLAD: Well, we'll drink from the jug. [*Raising the jug*] You're health, Christian!

ROMANIAN: And to you, Your Highness!

VLAD *is about to drink*

TURK: Don't drink, Sir, it's not wine.

VLAD: I know, it's poison, but it does me no harm. [*Drinks*] Your health too, Turk. It's through you that we Romanians are short of glasses. [*Drinks*] Ah! What a fine poison.

ROMANIAN: It quenches a thirst better than wine.

VLAD: [*To the Turk*] Your Romanian's very good!

TURK: I'm a native, not that it matters now.

VLAD: But it does.

TURK: For that matter I can also speak Persian, but I'll kick the bucket all the same. [*Dignified*] I'll die, but I shan't be sorry to do so, for I'll die at the hands of my own people and if your own people do it to you it's bound to be right.

VLAD: Even when they impale you? [*The Turk is silent. After a pause*] The sky is blue, the water, cold, and the cloud, dreamy. How do you say that in Turkish?

TURK: [*Answers him in Turkish*]

VLAD: I've got two apples, while my colleague Mohammed has two pears.

TURK: [*Translates*]

VLAD: [*Says something in Turkish*]

TURK: Not bad.

VLAD: [*Speaks another sentence in Turkish*] How's my accent?

TURK: Sounds like a real Turk, but what do you need to speak Turkish for?

VLAD: So I can have a talk with Mohammed.

DOMNICA: [*Enters carrying more food which she places on a table*] Uncle, you haven't eaten the roast chicken. Why, you've not even touched it!

VLAD: I've been too busy talking to my friend here.

ROMANIAN: [*To the Turk*] He says he's never touched it, yet half the spit's gone as well!

DOMNICA: [*Busying herself*] Try some! Look, this piece is done just right. You've got thinner lately. No wonder, when you eat with the dead. It's as if you only ate at funeral feasts. You should see how drawn your face is, yet your eyes are bright.

VLAD: I must be running a fever.

Enter PÎRVU *and* CHIORU, *two executioners. They drag in* JOIŢA

Scene 4

PÎRVU: I've caught a whore, Your Highness.

VLAD: Well, well!

JOIŢA: [*To Pîrvu*] Who are you calling whore, You've never screwed me in my life. Bastard, pig, bloody executioner. I hope you rot, stuck upside down on a stake, with the ravens pecking your eyes out. Get to Hell with you, you lousy, bloody wretch. Go on . . . drop dead! [*Spits on him. Turns to the Prince, incensed with rage*] Is there no justice left around here? How can you sit there like some dummy letting all the vagabonds strut around playing the emperor and making a mockery of everyone? I'd a good mind to grab a sword and hack 'em all to pieces.

VLAD: [*Laughing*] I like this woman!

JOIŢA: Every gypsy in fine feathers points the finger at us.

VLAD: And why do they do that, woman?

JOIŢA: For the food we've eaten and the fellows we've slept with . . .

VLAD: And who have you slept with, eh? Haven't you a husband?

JOIŢA: [*Weeping*] You can't call him a man, Your Highness.

VLAD: [*Calmly*] Why, what's wrong with him?

JOIŢA: [*Sobbing loudly*] He's a cripple.

PÎRVU: He lies in bed ill while she's had nine kids.

VLAD: Twins?

CHIORU: Not even that. One at a time.

VLAD: Is that right, woman?

JOIŢA: I had 'em from spite, Your Highness. Don't you go imagining it was fun! Just think, there was my man, ill in bed, no end to all the taxes he had to pay, nothing to be found, what else could we do, wretched women that we are? And besides we were always in terror of the Turks. One day they're coming, the next they're not! . . .

27

DOMNICA: Forgive her, Your Highness!

VLAD: You had best go away, dear.

DOMNICA: [*Kneeling*] Pardon her. [*Exits*]

VLAD: [*Rising*] And what is your opinion? Are they coming or not?

JOIȚA: Who, the Turks?

VLAD: Who else?

JOIȚA: Let 'em come, damn them, for they've been so bloody long they could have been at the back of beyond by now – off into Europe. Why should we be the only ones to resist them? And what do the people in the West do for us even though we defend them by standing our ground here? Stupid buggers!

VLAD: Who?

JOIȚA: The Turks of course.

VLAD: Why?

JOIȚA: They're only eager to fight us when they know they'll never defeat us. And it never dawns on them to attack you when your arses are out of your trousers!

PÎRVU: I'm sorry, Your Highness. There's nothing one can do about her foul language.

CHIORU: It's obscene.

JOIȚA: Obscene, my eye. Was your mother obscene having you! She'd have been better shoving out a pig!

CHIORU: Did you hear that?

VLAD: This woman deserves to live. At least she speaks her mind!

JOIȚA: Yes, I do. And I could say more, but I'm afraid. There are times when I keep my lips well buttoned.

VLAD: You'd do better to keep something else well buttoned. Why do you insist on whoring, bitch? Don't you know where your debauchery could land you? [*Solemnly*] Such times as these call for restraint. A people who let themselves be overcome by lust, who fling aside all restraint, are worthless and deserve to perish. I don't believe we're all vile and bad. That's why we're harsh with those who make it look as though we are. Even yesterday I punished a woman who had sent her husband off to war with a button missing off his shirt. She was a lazy bone-idle creature who never sewed his buttons on or did his buttonholes. How could such a soldier fight a war knowing that at home he had a lazy slut of a wife who never even sewed on his buttons? Now if you were a soldier's wife, carrying on with every Tom, Dick and Harry behind your husband's back just because he was crippled in the wars, how could men go willingly to war then, eh? Knowing what was in store for them the moment they returned crippled? Eh? How could they fight then?

JOIŢA: They'd have to win – or die!

VLAD: [*To the executioners*] Where are her bastards?

CHIORU: There, among the weeds [*Points at some place behind the scene*]

VLAD: [*Thinking it over*] I think we should pardon her, at least let her live.

JOIŢA: [*Falling to her knees*] Your Highness . . .

VLAD: Cut off her nipples . . .

JOIŢA: [*Shrieking*] No, no . . .

VLAD: . . . and nail on the hands of her bastards there instead.

JOIŢA: Oh, God!

VLAD: And then let her be carried like that from village to village so that all the people can see.

JOIŢA: [*Wailing and tearing her hair*] Have pity!

VLAD: As long as there are whores in this country, the Turks will be encouraged to rush in on us.

JOIŢA: Is it the Turks you're fighting or the Romanians? My little children, Lord, spare me . . .

VLAD: I don't only fight Turks. I also fight people like you and anyone else who brings grist to the Turks' mill.

Scene 5

In the distance there is a pipe playing. Vlad listens.

VLAD: [*Admiringly*] That's how all Romanians are – stubborn. They play their pipes whether they're happy or not. [*The pipe continues to play*] Yes, they certainly do. [*Turning to the two soldiers on the stakes*] Why aren't you two singing?

ROMANIAN: We don't feel like it.

TURK: We feel oppressed.

VLAD: Does it hurt?

ROMANIAN: Well . . .

VLAD: You should be happy now there's peace. [*Rubbing his hands*] Blessed be peace! You can concentrate on your own affairs. Now you know who you can rely on. You can always check out your own people but that's all over now. There's always an end to carefree living. Hard times are knocking at the door, lads. But what are you doing up there?

ROMANIAN: Just waiting, Your Highness.

VLAD: Waiting for what?

ROMANIAN: For the Last Judgement.

VLAD: Are you now? [*He remembers*] But tell me. Did you have a fair trial?

TURK: No!

ROMANIAN: They impaled us first, saying they'd try us afterwards. Some trial!

VLAD: Can you hang on a little longer? Wait for me. Don't die yet. I'll bring justice, Oh such justice I'll bring . . . if only I have enough time! [*Exits*]

Scene 6

VLAD *returns accompanied by* PAPUC, PÎRVU *and* CHIORU. *The latter two are carrying a huge stake across their shoulders.*

VLAD: [*Pointing to a spot between the two stakes standing on the stage*] Here. Put it in the middle.

PÎRVU: [*About to say something, then . . .*] Right in the middle?

VLAD: Right between the two of them. [*Pointing at the two soldiers*] On the same line, neither too much in front nor too much behind.

PÎRVU: [*To Chioru*] Follow a straight line. [*They start digging and thrusting the stake into the ground. Pîrvu is red in the face*] Can I ask who it's for?

VLAD: For one and all.

PÎRVU: [*Afraid*] One . . . and all?

VLAD: We're keeping it here in its place . . . vacant . . . for you, Papuc, for you're no saint, and for you and you too, for all of you. Any of us might err one day. So let's have a vacant stake, right here. Some day it'll come in handy. [*To the executioners*] Drive it in . . . straight! [*To Papuc*] Come along. [VLAD *and* PAPUC *exit*]

CHIORU: [*To Pîrvu*] We must keep a straight line.

The two busy themselves with the stake, driving it well into the ground with slow expert thrusts. The scene is played in silence.

30

ACT
TWO

Evening

PART ONE

Scene 1

The Prince's Court

The throne in the state-room. VLAD *is on his throne in his rich state robes. On his head he wears a fur cap adorned with precious stones and an osprey feather.*

THE PAINTER: [*Having mixed some colours*] Just a little . . . to the right . . . Now look this way. [*Pointing somewhere behind him. Painting*] You have a restless nature. It's rather difficult to get your head . . .

VLAD: [*Under his breath*] So they say . . .

THE PAINTER: Would you mind not blinking. The expression in your eyes is terrifying. Can I speak openly? I'm rather afraid of looking straight into your eyes . . . so big.

VLAD: A sour or a sweet tongue makes them grow even bigger.

THE PAINTER: I get the olive tint of the skin only by using an earth colour that one find's here. Perhaps that's why Your Highness is nicknamed The Devil.

VLAD: [*Driving away an insect with his hand*] Can't I even catch a glow-worm? For if I sit here idle without catching some minute insect it means I've wasted away. Don't paint me looking wasted on that canvas.

THE PAINTER: [*Laughing*] You're fond of words with double meanings. It's the same with His Most Serene Highness Mohammed, the greatest conqueror in the world. By the way, he didn't conquer me. I made his portrait, which hangs in his palace in Constantinople. Perhaps one day you'll have the opportunity of seeing it.

VLAD: I regret I shan't be travelling that far . . .

THE PAINTER: [*Secretly*] I'm afraid he plans to come to see your portrait.

33

VLAD: Is it worth the effort?

THE PAINTER: [*Laughing*] He's very inquisitive and very fond of . . . heads in oil . . . and like you he may be joking or he may not. It was there that I first heard of Vlad. I was working near the Sultan's throne when your brother came into the room . . . he has permission to enter at will . . . a great privilege. [*Purposely*] He's a very handsome man.

VLAD: Radu is handsome . . . yes, I'll say that for him.

THE PAINTER: But he is not over-fond of you. He'd like to be the reigning prince here. And I have a feeling that one day he will be.

VLAD: Daring our drawn swords?

THE PAINTER: He'll try. The Sultan spoils him.

VLAD: I know.

THE PAINTER: He said that he doubted you could ever be faithful to the Sultan and that you'd be waiting for the right opportunity to rebel.

VLAD: [*Non-committal*] I happen to be on the best of terms with the Sublime Porte.

THE PAINTER: [*Continuing to paint*] Mohammed's clever. He reads between the lines and he's a military genius. Now that he's taken up residence in Constantinople, I can't imagine what could stand in his way.

VLAD: [*Dryly*] We could.

THE PAINTER: [*Startled*] Who?

VLAD: We could, honourable master.

THE PAINTER: You haven't said yet whether I can speak openly or not. Artists are never interesting unless they speak out. The world teems with sycophants, but they can never boast the status of an artist. I am no politician. I just travel from place to place and from one country to another painting portraits of monarchs. [*Laughing*] Artistic monarchomania. I've learned a great deal and like to chat about them, freely . . . I only know you from hearsay. I haven't quite been able to make out your face. Still, I can ascertain some lines of your destiny which seem to me quite fantastic and I am deeply moved that you do me the honour of sitting for me for a minute a day.

VLAD: You can think freely and say whatever you want to say, nobody's going to chop your head off for it.

THE PAINTER: Beheading's becoming quite fashionable now, so it's no longer very interesting. But what was I saying? Oh yes, Mohammed's army is huge. An army almost a 150,000 strong

34

took part in the storming of the Byzantine stronghold. [*Secretly*] And do you know? Not a single soldier was sent home . . . Can Wallachia be such an obstacle?

VLAD: I am the Sultan's vassal.

THE PAINTER: Only apparently so, and if I might give you a piece of advice: keep up appearances! The Sultan knows the eyes of the world are upon him and the slightest sign of subordination would be considered as a personal insult. If you were ever to throw down the gauntlet, you should be prepared to defy lightning itself.

VLAD: [*Thoughtfully*] Heaven alone knows what the outcome will be.

THE PAINTER: On what does Your Highness rely? You found the army in utter chaos. The boyars are against you. They say you make a show of cruelty and that your aim is to be all-powerful, that you've already started to rid the country of the best of the boyars.

VLAD: To prevent them from consorting with rogues and thieves.

THE PAINTER: Such things are unforgivable.

VLAD: [*Casually*] You don't happen to go in for politics do you?

THE PAINTER: Oh no, no . . .

VLAD: Yet you're very well informed!

THE PAINTER: Painting . . . It develops naturally with us . . . Just a moment while I mix some more colours . . .

Enter PAPUC

Scene 2

THE PAINTER: [*Continuing*] This earth you call loam becomes very gluey when kneaded following a recipe of mine. If only we had such colours we could create paintings that would last for centuries . . . In any case, much better than yours. Why hasn't the fresco developed here if you've got such natural resources?

VLAD: All the peasants have the fresco stuck to the soles of their feet. [*Solemnly*] At the moment we support the walls with our own arms. When everyone stops battering the wall in an attempt to demolish it, we'll find work for the fresco painters to do.

THE PAINTER: Are they in prison?

VLAD: They're in the army. Preparing the loam you like so well. Pounding it with their feet. That should knead it well enough, don't you think? [*To Papuc*] Well?

PAPUC: There's someone who is refusing to pay his taxes. A lunatic.

VLAD: Why does he refuse to pay? We must examine the reason. It might uncover a more general evil which we may be able to put right.

PAPUC: His ideas are all up the pole. They don't conform to our times. I tell you, he's mad. He says he doesn't live in Your Highness's era and that he wouldn't live in it, not for the world . . . He does not like the times as they are.

VLAD: What?

PAPUC: He says he lives a hundred years ago. He's one brick short of a full load!

VLAD: [*Laughing*] What's his business here?

PAPUC: [*Afraid*] His wife sent him on in advance to see how things are. She's pregnant and wants to know whether she should give birth to the child or poison herself.

VLAD: He must be imagining things . . . Let's have a look at him . . .

PAPUC *goes out*

Scene 3

THE PAINTER: In times of stress religious fanaticism often rears its head. You see, it's one way of protesting. Forgive me for prying a little . . .

VLAD: Here I am trying to discipline a gang of thieves. I've already noted everything you've said. [*Bursting out*] Here I am, Lord over these forests, teeming with thieves, over dangerous roads full of ruts and holes, and over a starving disorganised army.

THE PAINTER: I didn't mean to upset you . . . but . . . my paints have been stolen!

VLAD: You can get more here.

THE PAINTER: Yes, but they're no good. They discolour the moment they touch the canvas . . . as if out of sheer fright. I did send to Padua for some more, but the coach was waylaid near Bucharest and my man was butchered.

36

VLAD: [*Bursts out laughing*] Well, who would believe it!

Enter PAPUC *bringing in* MINICA

Scene 4

PAPUC: This is the fellow.

VLAD: What era do you live in, man?

MINICA: I don't know, it's all so muddled . . . There are great quarrels. Heads are being chopped off. And no one knows yet who's going to win.

VLAD: What year is it?

MINICA: One thousand, three hundred and fifty nine.

THE PAINTER: So you're exactly one hundred years behind the times. How fortunate to be able to travel like that down the centuries.

MINICA: Well, it's the Blessed Virgin that's granted me this . . .

THE PAINTER: Ah, I see it all now. You've got free passage down the ways of the Lord!

VLAD: All right. So be it, but why didn't you pay your taxes?

MINICA: What, pay a hundred years in advance? I'm not mad, you know!

VLAD: Tell me something. Who am I?

MINICA: Vlad. But everyone calls you the Impaler, and please don't be angry with me for telling you so.

VLAD: So . . . you acknowledge that I am the ruling monarch.

PAPUC: Your Highness, you're wasting your time.

VLAD: Never mind. Now the reigning prince of the land should be acknowledged by every single citizen. [*To Minica*] Do you acknowledge me as the reigning prince of Wallachia?

VLAD: Yes, but only a hundred years hence. Until then, well, we'll see . . . [*Sighing*] What's going to happen now?

VLAD: [*Hardly able to suppress his laughter*] How did you manage to find me here?

MINICA: My wife – she's pregnant – says, 'You go on ahead and see how things are. For I've five children already and all dead.' The pagans first and now our own people have hacked at them alive. So I'd rather take some potion or other instead of bringing yet another child into this world. You'll not catch me at it again. It's over and . . . ' [*He begins to weep*] Five children. Do you know how it feels to lose five children and all on account of history?

VLAD: Well, now you've seen how things stand. What are you going to tell your wife?

MINICA: Will I ever get back to her?

VLAD: Why not. You can return the same way you came. [*Paternally*] Go home, have your child christened, have a good booze up and then make love to your wife.

MINICA: She'll never do it when I tell her what I've seen around here.

VLAD: We need more people. Let them live and multiply.

MINICA: Your Highness, I've seen the stakes. I've heard the groans of tortured Romanians. [*Reproachfully*] How could you do such things?

VLAD: Perhaps you've imagined it all . . . eaten some rich food that's disagreed with you, given you nightmares.

MINICA: What nightmares? [*Falls to his knees*] Your Highness, let me . . .

VLAD: Now what do you want?

MINICA: Let me stay here. I'm tired of travelling. How could I have the heart to go all that way back?

VLAD: If you do stay, you'll have to pay taxes.

MINICA: [*Crying*] Pay taxes for a hundred years hence?

VLAD: [*Patiently*] And what should I do with you? Keep you here to put strange ideas into my courtiers' heads?

MINICA: No, no, for I don't want to live in your time. You'd better . . .

VLAD: . . . . skin you alive?

MINICA: It doesn't matter. It's not as if we haven't been skinned alive already by all of them – many times before.

VLAD: What do you mean. By all of them?

MINICA: All the princes who ever sided with me or against me. All of them before you, Your Highness. They've all skinned me alive time and time again. For I kept telling them I didn't like the times and then whang . . . off goes my head . . . See these scars here! [*He unbuttons his shirt at the neck*]

VLAD: All right, I believe you. I'm sorry there's nothing left for me to . . . whang [*He indicates chopping off a head*] as those before have already done it.

MINICA: Oh but there is, but death has no power over me now. God gave me this power; the power to keep on dying for no purpose at all. [*He rises*]

PAPUC: [*Stares at the Prince*] Hacked to pieces? To bits?

MINICA: No, all the others said exactly the same . . . to Hell with it . . . they cut your head off and blood gushes out . . . just the same. Well, what do you want? Am I to stay on here?

VLAD: Your wife's expecting you back.

MINICA: [*Weeping*] I can't tell her what I've seen. She'll miscarry. And I badly want a son. Well, perhaps it'd be better for me to go on higher up in the hills. You see, I started in the valley and kept on walking and walking and yet it gets worse and worse. If only I could get to the top of the mountain and see all that beauty then I could yell for joy.

VLAD: So you'd like to walk on and on and get nowhere.

MINICA: Just as long as my feet will carry me. On and on and on . . .

VLAD: And leave all of us here to get on with the times.

MINICA: Everyone should bide his own time . . .

VLAD: And where are you going to stop now?

MINICA: In the year 1600. I don't know what makes me think it's going to be all right in 1600.

VLAD: And what don't you like about our time?

MINICA: [*Evasively*] Well . . .

THE PAINTER: Speak out, nobody's going to chop your head off.

MINICA: I don't like . . . the situation. It stinks. It stinks so bad that you don't know what the devil to do about it. I've already said to your people that that's how it is. Just pretend you don't notice I said, and that you see nothing.

VLAD: Yes, but I who am responsible for everything, what should I do?

MINICA: [*Laughing*] Pretend . . . you haven't noticed anything.

VLAD: [*Laughing*] You've saved your neck from the axe. I shan't condemn you. God speed you well and if you ever do utter that yell of joy, your wife won't be the only one to rejoice. How pregnant is she?

MINICA: Six months . . . a hundred years ago, that is she'll have it soon, but she's waiting for me to report back, to see whether women can still bear children in Wallachia. [*Sighs*]

PAPUC: You're like a holy pilgrim on his way to the future, to a holy shrine better than life.

MINICA: That's right. A pilgrim always on the lookout to do a bad

39

turn but never finding it.

VLAD: Perhaps you'll find it one day . . . as for me, I want to find it now. Let's all find it now.

MINICA: [*Vexed*] What, with things as they are?

VLAD: We can't all rush over hedges and ditches. My plans are for the present, under these circumstances. It's true I myself don't like them, but I'm the reigning prince, and unlike you I can't be too choosy where history's concerned. I owe it to my people to stay in the present and try to make it good, so good that we'd all leap from our bodies with joy.

MINICA: I've brought along the tools.

VLAD: What tools?

MINICA: I couldn't bear the thought of any other death. If they've chopped off my head once, at least let me die the same death again and again. I don't want to be skinned alive, impaled or imprisoned, for I get so muddled.

VLAD: You can go! We'll not touch you, for politically speaking you don't exist. And, practically speaking, even if we did harm you nothing would change. [*Laughing*] In fact there's not much harm in sending an envoy into the future. [*Picks up his block and axe and puts them back into the bag. To Papuc*] Let him go free and let none harm him. He's our man. Our envoy.

MINICA: It's hard on me and on you too. Your Highness [*About to go*]

VLAD: [*Giving him a purse with some money*] Take it. It's a gift from me. As for the taxes, you'll have to pay those . . . It's the law.

MINICA: [*Takes one coin only*] I'll just take this . . . then you'll make a bit of a loss. [*Goes out followed by Papuc*]

Scene 5

VLAD: I said to all the executioners, quite clearly, that cruelty – that is, cruel deeds – have to be done by the light of the sun, but that reasons must be made clear. Yet I seem to be preaching to the wilderness. And then just one individual wrongs both the prince and the system. [*Thoughtfully*] Here I sit, talking even to ghosts.

THE PAINTER: A reigning prince should listen with both ears.

VLAD: Giving his right ear to the living and his left ear to the dead.

THE PAINTER: What I appreciate here is the novelty. New

sensations . . . right and left . . . [*Secretly*] Tell me, is my life safe here at Your Highness's court? It would be such a shame for the portrait not to . . . I pin great hopes on this portrait. Never before have I found such an interesting model. I don't usually flatter people – you've probably noticed that already – but this time I feel I'm experiencing something artistically unique. You know there is a theory of charismatic eyes . . . in any case I feel quite attached to Your Highness by a sort of sympathy that's hard to define. As a matter of fact, in a way we're sort of kinsmen. [*Laughing*] Common ancestry. One of your soldiers said to me only the other day, 'What's the difference between Trajan and Decebal? We have to honour them both.'

VLAD: You're very lucky that you're not my brother. I mean Radu in the Turkish Empire. Did you know I spent my youth there? I was a hostage! I had the opportunity of meeting some Italian artists and this made me look favourably upon the attitude you take. An attitude which is invariably provocative. You're a strange lot, you artists.

THE PAINTER: Artists should not be exterminated . . .

VLAD: It would be a little difficult to do so. Everyone in this country creates songs and we'd be lord over . . . nothing but stakes. So we go on pardoning . . . Though, mind you, not all the songs are good ones.

THE PAINTER: I think I've succeeded in painting the mouth. I intend to make two portraits if I have enough paint. One for you and one I'll take back to my own country. [*Pained*] Works of art get lost here or else they're systematically destroyed. It's the same with the Turks. If I tried to sell your portrait to them, it'd be hacked to pieces. I dare say the same would happen to the portrait of the Sultan. [*Vlad laughs*] Now it's different with us in Italy. There, there are great art collectors like the Pope, who would pay handsomely for a portrait in oils representing the Prince of Wallachia. And its value would increase even more if . . . heaven forbid, facing the Turks alone, you lost the battle. Ah, you've moved!

VLAD: I can't waste any more time sitting here. I'm sorry.

THE PAINTER: I'm very grateful that Your Highness allowed me to work such a long time in his presence.

VLAD: I like to converse with people from time to time. Unfortunately, I shan't be available for the next few days.

THE PAINTER: I see I'm dismissed. Forgive me if I angered you.

VLAD: Not at all. Please stay at my court as long as you please and if you are afraid about what will happen . . . and if we are able to keep our head on our shoulders . . . you may be able to complete the portrait.

THE PAINTER: [*Happily*] I'll follow you anywhere, even onto the field.

VLAD: [*Laughing*] You're a very courageous master painter. May the Lord protect you and add health to the courage you already possess.

The painter bows and exits

Scene 6

VLAD: All dressed up like a corpse . . . sitting for my portrait! Whenever I don these robes I seem to be lying alive in a coffin. No wonder in some parts of the country a coffin's called a throne. [*Relaxing onto the throne*] That's how it is, then. Seated in a coffin which others want to unseat. All princely offspring with a right to princely rewards. For the time being the duty of a good manager is to weed his garden. Those who shelter our enemies are no doubt enemies themselves. I don't feel like starting work on the pagans until I've finished with our relatives and the Christians [*Makes as if to impale them*]. We fight in the old-fashioned way . . . from the side-lines. We know where we stand!

Enter DOMNICA

Scene 7

VLAD: Leave me or I shall lose track of my thoughts. No – stay. Come and look at this coffin. Is it smeared with honey? [*Rises from his throne and pretends to examine it carefully*]

DOMNICA: [*Laughing*] It's a throne. The throne of the country. How could it be smeared with honey? It'd stick to your bottom.

VLAD: Then why do they all buzz round it like wasps? Why does everyone want to sit on it?

DOMNICA: How should I know?

VLAD: I was just talking to myself. A few moments ago I too wanted to sit on it and . . . you know what? Smear it with tar . . . so that we'd all be free from temptation . . . And then put a stool nearby for me to sit on.

DOMNICA: But you're a prince. You're expected to sit on the throne.

VLAD: I am, but I want to be different and then see if the painter still pesters me.

DOMNICA: That painter? Throw him out, Your Highness. [*Ashamed*] He's too free with his words.

VLAD: What?

DOMNICA: He told me I should wear low-necked blouses [*Pointing to her decollette*] and that he wanted to paint my portrait. [*Crosses herself*] He said he's never seen such a beauty and that [*Crying*] I should pose for him nude.

VLAD: [*Laughing*] While he asked me to wear my thickest clothes as if it was mid-winter. The sly dog, and said he'd never seen anyone quite like me before.

DOMNICA: I shall go to a nunnery . . . making a fool of me as if I were one of those . . . wantons [*Loud sobs*]

VLAD: You're a good girl. You didn't take off your clothes. But I am a dissolute man for I dressed the way he wanted me to. However, it's over now. [*Turns the throne with its front to the wall*] Now remember! Smear it with tar!

DOMNICA: . . . And desecrate it? Your father once sat there. All those proud princes did. Let's keep it, for appearances' sake. For some envoy who might arrive . . . and for other purposes too. Why should we dirty it? It'd be such a pity. It's rosewood.

VLAD: All right then . . . but don't forget to fetch me that three-legged stool. Go on now.

DOMNICA: [*Hesitating*] I was thinking . . . Perhaps he didn't really mean any harm.

VLAD: Who?

DOMNICA: The master painter. Send him back home, but alive.

VLAD: Very well.

DOMNICA: Don't poison him.

VLAD: We'll see. Go on now. [*She exits*] Girls of today! They may be good, but if they're not guarded with a broomstick they catch fire!

43

PART TWO

Scene 1

In the forest. A ravine

DAN: [*Shaking off the dust and undergrowth from his clothes*] Isn't it strange . . . all those nooks and crannies of history! All your life you slither like snakes in the dust and when you do finally emerge, lifting up your head, someone comes along to dig you a grave.

TENEA: Now let's not be prophets of doom. Your Highness . . .

DAN: Your Highness, is it? Ha! Ha! But not yet! [*Tenea bows low to him*] There where earth and sky meet, that's a ravine . . . and it's there where our vast horizon lies. [*Looks about him*] Not a bad hiding place is it? I managed to get by well enough. How about you?

TENEA: But you're forgetting. I'm his counsellor! All I have to say is, 'I'm off to fight the dragons of the desert.' [*Secretively*] Everyone's getting anxious now. The Captains are all desperately looking for spies, traitors and those who shun honest work and love of their country.

DAN: Idle gossip.

TENEA: Perhaps . . . but they're certainly on our tracks . . . I have to pretend I'm trying to find out who or what I am . . . so that I don't find myself, so that they don't find me.

DAN: Go on! What are you talking about. You're like quick silver.

TENEA: I know, but it's not the big one who's our worst enemy . . . It's Papuc.

DAN: What, aren't you sitting day in day out, cheek to jowl, shaping the destiny of this country?

TENEA: So it appears, but Papuc bars everything. He puts his spokes in everything.

DAN: [*Impatiently*] Papuc! Papuc! That's all I ever hear. I'm sick to

44

death of him. All any of you do is to moan that he's forever standing in your way.

TENEA: So he does . . .

DAN: I don't want to interfere . . . but . . . [*Thoughtfully*] Doesn't he ever eat mushrooms?

TENEA: Who, Papuc?

DAN: Of course.

TENEA: No.

DAN: How stupid of you to let all your riches go to waste. It wasn't that long ago that poison could satisfy every glutton in the place. Many gave up the ghost so readily . . . disappearing in no time at all, just like dandelion clocks blown by the wind.

TENEA: Well, it's no use. He doesn't like mushrooms.

DAN: Well, that's your affair. Now we, who come from foreign parts are not supposed to compose the menu! Oh, stop complaining! [*Changing the tone of his voice*] Men, confusion is the key-word. So dig . . . a precipice.

TENEA: [*Smiling*] Don't worry. We're still digging from inside the ravine.

DAN: Create chaos. Dig on!

TENEA: [*Musing*] How? Hand to mouth? Everything's already confused . . . there's chaos everywhere. [*Annoyed*] But it never lasts long. Along come his men and spoil it all by putting things right.

DAN: Then put more heart and soul in it lads, more heart and soul.

TENEA: I do my best [*Afraid*] I'm afraid. The prince has started to dole out justice in one direction and now he's reached the other side of the forest. Your Highness, when my turn comes, will he think twice before turning his violence on me?

DAN: [*Trying to encourage him*] On you? Stop being such a fool!

TENEA: He's got a heavy hand . . . he used to joust . . . eyes piercing . . . mind sharp. [*Kneeling*] Oh Lord, bring the army faster!

DAN: [*Composed*] Are you referring to me or the Lord in Heaven?

TENEA: Oh, save us Lord!

DAN: Why do you hate him so much?

TENEA: It's Papuc. He always looks at me sideways. He squints, you know. Oh, if I could only squeeze him a bit in my arms. That would soon cure his squint and make him eye me properly at last. Do you know what they've thought up now?

DAN: [*Eagerly*] No, what?

45

TENEA: To move the country seat.

DAN: What, from Tîrgovişte? Good God, where to?

TENEA: To a village, the village of Tucur . . . or is it Ciucur . . . Ciucureşti or Bucureşti? [*Annoyed*] A sheepfold! A mere pen! A shepherd's pen! It's not even a market town, like Cetatea de Floci . . . some fleece!

DAN: I hear there are fine women there with plenty of fleece on them. [*Laughs*]

TENEA: [*Not hearing him*] And yet you wonder why I hate him? When there's not a seat left in its proper place.

DAN: [*Haughtily*] We milk him one way . . . with pen and ink. Telling tales! But the Saxons are demanding a great deal of money for them. I don't pay them word by word as they do in the West. I pay them letter by letter! I gave them money. What else was there to do? [*Sighing*] Paying taxes on Gutenburg! You see, I'll put an end to it the minute I step on the throne. I'll not publish a single book! We'll become civilized first . . . stressing one thing at a time. We'll have to rely on either the peasants or else the boyars . . . I'm not sure which yet . . . The boyars might be better because they're all on our side and we couldn't possibly lose . . . and I've noticed that Vlad suspects the lot of them.

TENEA: You'll be saving Wallachia from this deadlock she's in.

DAN: And Moldavia. For I shan't lift one finger unless it affects both countries. How's Stefanache?

TENEA: The whole of Suceava's mourning one minute and rejoicing the next. If they're not in the cellars they're making merry in the ramparts. The boyars there have started muttering amongst themselves, while the prince shouts . . . off with their heads! [*Secretively*] In every county there's a massacre and you see, Moldavia won't put up with him for much longer . . . a month or two at the most . . . no more.

DAN: There are rumours like that here too . . . that a prince such as him can't possibly stay on the throne for much longer. His military prospects are no better either. What about Raducu?

TENEA: Still in Istanbul . . . wearing long hair and baggy trousers!

DAN: He's obsessed with the Turks, but he's wrong. We'll only form an alliance with the Germans. They're the only ones to offer any guarantee in this present situation in Europe. We'll make a shield of Vienna and mind our own business.

TENEA: That's not a bad idea, but who's going to pay?

DAN: Pay whom?

TENEA: The Germans?

DAN: The Turks!

TENEA: [*Puzzled*] The Turks?

DAN: The Turks will pay them tribute and us as well.

TENEA: [*Aside*] Is he mocking me or gone mad? [*Aloud*] Europe's in such a state. Sir . . . that . . . your Highness! Such a mess!

DAN: That we'll unravel. But we need to find a country to finance us.

TENEA: But which country?

DAN: Which country? Ours of course. Wallachia.

TENEA: [*Scratching his head*] Well, we'll see . . . [*Aside*] What the hell does this damned adventurer want to do?

DAN: Now don't be afraid, you old fox. We're just seeing which way the wind blows.

TENEA: [*Calmly*] Well, that's enough. I feel better now.

DAN: You're not clever enough to play first fiddle. That job's for those born in Cremona.

TENEA: [*Fails to understand*] Where? Of course. Well, I'm off.

DAN: You're only fit to play second fiddle.

TENEA: Where? Yes, that's all I'm fit for! [*Produces a slip of paper*] I've put it all down on this. I've been going over it in my mind night after night.

DAN: [*Looking at the paper*] I hope you don't intend to sell us out!

TENEA: [*Offended*] What us? How could you think . . .

DAN: [*Cruelly*] Ah, that first foot wrong . . . we know how much you love your family, so we'll keep them near us just a little longer. They're well guarded. But the first suspicious move on your part –

TENEA: [*Bursting out*] Your Highness! Do you think I stay here because of my family or ardent patriotism?

DAN: I don't know what to believe!

TENEA: I don't understand what's going on. I've no head for politics . . . I'm just fit to play second fiddle. All you wanted to do was put me to the test.

DAN: Why? It's your wife I put to the test.

TENEA: And did she withstand it?

DAN: Yes, she did. The way all women withstand a test. She gave in. Towards the end they put up more resistance and then – yield again . . .

TENEA: [*Aside*] I'll kill him! Do I undermine the Prince's authority merely for this adventurer. Feeling the sword of Damocles

47

hanging over my head as I do? [*Aloud*] Well, that's how things
are. She's old enough. I shan't hang onto her skirts. She can
look after herself.

DAN: A minute ago you wanted to kill me, didn't you?

TENEA: Yes.

DAN: Well, I shouldn't try if I were you, for I am wearing a coat of
mail. Perhaps you were unaware that you'd fallen into my
clutches. It only needs one of my men to let a word drop and
Vlad will make you pay for it. [*A rustling sound*] What's that?

TENEA: My men. We're in this together.

DAN: Then let's be sensible. [*In a different tone*] Look brother, why
don't we behave like brothers?

TENEA: [*Appeased*] Well, we could be in for trouble brother. If we
start murdering each other, we shall be giving Vlad a free hand.

DAN: You're right.

TENEA: Does Your Highness have a plan? Or haven't you thought
it all out yet?

DAN: We'll wait and see. And I will follow your advice. Keep to my
side, but . . . a few steps behind us!

TENEA: [*Anxiously*] Five or six. I do realize I mustn't be too
conspicuous.

DAN: There's something I need to know. Why did the Pope send
that painter as a spy to Vlad's Court? Why not a sculptor or an
architect?

TENEA: God knows! He probably thought we don't build much,
and we're not ripe enough to start building statues. But how do
you know he's a spy?

DAN: The Pope himself. Go and tell him this. 'We need a portrait of
the Prince, in the Italian style. Deadline tonight.' Don't go into
any details. If he works for the Pope he may as well work for us too.

TENEA: Splendid! Your logic and judgement are magnificent!

DAN: That's just the start. When I mount the throne I shall have
everything I'll ever need right there at my disposal. [*In a
changed tone*] Some say he's dark and others that he's fair.

TENEA: Who?

DAN: The Prince. The emperor in Vienna and the head of the
Butcher's Guild at Braşov both said to me, 'Sir, what does he
look like, for he's terrified the whole world.' So I said, 'Well
what can I say? Some say he's tall and gaunt as a greyhouse,
others that he's short-necked, stocky, and broad-shouldered
with the eyes of a hawk!'

TENEA: It's difficult to describe him in just a few words.

DAN: Everything's agreed then. We paint his portrait on a target and set a prize of a few guns on his head. The man who brings him to us, dead or alive – gets the guns.

TENEA: [*Thoughtfully*] Can those in his retinue also compete?

DAN: Leave it ambiguous. All in good time. Just ask the Italian to do the portrait.

TENEA: The truth is he's not a spy. He's the Prince's friend and madly in love with one of his relations. She's very attractive.

DAN: Really? Then let's speed things up a bit.

TENEA: We need an army, Your Highness. In fifteenth century Wallachia you can't rape a virgin without an army. [*Laughs. Dan also laughs. Noises are heard nearby. Tenea is calm*] My men. Out looking for pretenders!

DAN: [*Drawing his knife*] Traitor!

TENEA: Be careful! I'm also wearing a coat of mail! [*Takes out his dagger*]

Enter GÅGÅUȚÅ *in a hurry*

GÅGÅUȚÅ: [*Afraid*] Papuc! With a whole troop of horsemen.

TENEA: Who's betrayed us?

GÅGÅUȚÅ: [*Tearing at his hair*] The climate, brothers, the climate! The climate's so rotten it makes the Prince suspicious. Be careful. Papuc has nothing definite on us yet.

TENEA: [*To Dan*] You see? Are we still brothers?

DAN: Yes.

TENEA: And when you do come . . . I'll be the first to play second fiddle . . . only five steps behind.

DAN: If Mohammed wants to be the first to kill him, he can, but he'll have to put it in writing so my country will be free once again.

TENEA: There's an entrance to the cave by that rock over there. Go and follow the stream until you come out into the daylight. [*The noises appear nearer*] Quick! Quick!

DAN: Don't forget the portrait! [*Exit*]

TENEA: Risking our lives for people like him!

GÅGÅUȚÅ: Yes, but he's of noble descent. He promised us promotion. He'll help the boyars, levy new taxes so that soon the people will have nothing and all will be in order. [*Dreaming*] The whole country will look like a flower-bed with just one flower. [*Startled*] Papuc!

49

PAPUC: Is that you, Tenea? What are you doing with the knife? Not
suicidal I hope?

TENEA: Just a bear. It went off in that direction.

PAPUC: Bear hunting comes later. Extermination of other beasts
comes first. We'll go to the Birsa Land to root out Dan's army
as it prepares to invade. No, you stay here. You must be tired.

Scene 2

Night in the Prince's Palace

VLAD: Yes, that really was a comet. We've got problems with the
sky as well. [*After a moment*] Have we any astronomers?

PAPUC: Yes, we have.

VLAD: You don't seem very sure?

PAPUC: We have, but they're not very efficient. [*Secretively*] Not
very productive.

VLAD: Have your astronomers discovered any new stars?

PAPUC: Not one.

VLAD: Then what do they do all day long?

PAPUC: They sit around idle all day, saying there's nothing they can
see in daylight. But at night . . .

VLAD: At night?

PAPUC: They doze, feel bored, make pipes, create prayers to St.
Anthony . . . and gossip. You can't imagine what gossips they
are, these scientists of the sky. I had to force one of them to
climb down from the platform . . .

VLAD: From what?

PAPUC: A platform. Up a tree . . . that's where they work.

VLAD: You mean where they *sit*.

PAPUC: Well, in a manner of speaking they 'work'. There is a
platform in a tree and they climb a ladder and stare at the sky.
I've often warned them that I'll take the ladder away if they
keep being late.

VLAD: How many of them are there?

PAPUC: Fifteen. Well, now there are only fourteen because I made
one climb down. He said it was no good without any women

whether in the sky, on earth or in between . . .

VLAD: Who's in charge?

PAPUC: A man called Dragavei. A beefy fellow. Like an oak! A good man . . . big, strong . . . That's what makes me wonder why on earth we need such well-built astronomers?! When it comes to fighting a battle, it's only the feeble ones that . . .

VLAD: Send him here. I hope he is up the tree.

PAPUC: Yes, they're all there. All at their observation post. [*Goes out but quickly returns*] I've given the orders.

VLAD: [*Pacing the room*] You say the Turks are already on the way?

PAPUC: Not at the moment, but I'm informed they're considering it . . .

VLAD: Are the men who informed you reliable?

PAPUC: The cream. They spot everything.

VLAD: What's happening about Poienari?

PAPUC: What, the Citadel?

VLAD: Yes.

PAPUC: I have asked. They said they'd start work after St. Ilie's day.

VLAD: Why after . . . ? It's May now!

PAPUC: Who knows? That's what they said.

VLAD: Tomorrow morning we'll go to church. There is a service and then we'll all dash to Poienari and gather up all the soldiers. We'll dig new ditches, make bricks, carry stones. We'll set them in a line on the hill and pass them hand to hand.

PAPUC: But tomorrow's Easter. The people go to church.

VLAD: Fine . . . That means they'll be in one spot. We'll find them there and take them with us to build up the citadel.

PAPUC: Surely we could start the day after tomorrow.

VLAD: Too late.

PAPUC: The villagers will be in their Sunday best!

VLAD: What is more sacred than building a citadel on Easter Day; to knead clay for bricks and work until your clothes turn to rags. That's what a feast day means. Do you know what a citadel really means, Papuc?

Enter the astronomer DRAGAVEI:

51

Scene 3

DRAGAVEI *bows to the Prince*

VLAD: Are you the astronomer?

DRAGAVEI: Yes. I am astrologer Dragavei . . .

VLAD: Your eyes are almost closed. Are you tired?

DRAGAVEI: Don't worry about my eyes. In our profession they close themselves.

VLAD: Did you see the phenomenon?

DRAGAVEI: What phenomenon?

PAPUC: [*Helping him out*] A star with a tail. A comet appeared in the sky just now . . .

DRAGAVEI: Oh that. Yes, of course I saw it.

VLAD: What was it like?

DRAGAVEI: Well it had a tail . . . that long.

VLAD: What do you mean?

DRAGAVEI: That long. [*Gestures with his hands*]

VLAD: Was it blue, green, grey? Did it leave a trail behind, of iron filings, sulphur or lead? What was it like?

DRAGAVEI: [*Disconcerted*] To tell you the truth, I . . . I didn't see it for myself. I happened to be looking in the other direction.

VLAD: [*Clapping his hands in surprise*] Well, well! Did you hear that, Papuc? He was looking in the other direction! There's a comet in the sky once every hundred years and our astronomers are looking in the opposite direction. At some woman no doubt!

DRAGAVEI: You see . . . we have divided the sky into sections. Each is delegated to watch that particular part. Everything is then observed and duly noted down. Every small detail. [*Proudly*] No comet crossed my section.

VLAD: Then whose section did it cross?

DRAGAVEI: [*Sadly*] It was Mierlusca's.

VLAD: And what did Mierlusca report to you, his boss?

DRAGAVEI: Nothing. He was dismissed. [*Motions reproachfully to Papuc*] So as he was no longer looking at the sky, his section wasn't covered . . . and at that very moment the phenomenon occurred.

VLAD: [*Laughing*] What do you know? No one noticed it! Well, as it happens, we did notice it, so that the comet will not be able to boast it passed over Wallachia without anyone seeing it. Listen, when such things are due to occur why don't you inform people a few days in advance? That's why I summoned you here.

DRAGAVEI: But how could we let you know? Such things are the secrets of the universe. Nobody knows. Nobody can learn such things.

VLAD: How is it then that others manage to learn at least one week in advance?

DRAGAVEI: [*Laughing*] Others? You must mean a week later!

VLAD: No. In advance. [*Seriously*] Why don't you work like scientists?

DRAGAVEI: [*Determined*] We haven't any reels. We've asked time and time again. They've promised, we've asked, they've promised . . . and so far . . . nothing!

PAPUC: [*Guiltily*] It is our fault. We'll see to it they get what they need.

DRAGAVEI: [*Plucking up courage*] Now if only we had reels, we could save our eyesight by peering through the holes.

VLAD: Because you failed to see the comet, for the time being we'll just cut off that tail between your legs . . . !

DRAGAVEI: [*Falling to his knees*] Your Highness!

PAPUC: Shall we geld him as well?

DRAGAVEI: No, don't cripple me. I've asked repeatedly to be sent to the army. I swear to God I've always wanted to fight for Your Highness! They forced me to climb that platform. I'd rather dance with a dead Turk between my teeth than . . .

PAPUC: He is very brave. He did once dance with a dead Turk between his teeth.

VLAD: Why did he leave the army?

PAPUC: You know . . . his father . . . a father's love . . . he begged us to . . .

VLAD: [*In kinder tones*] Astronomer! You despicable parasite and layabout.

DRAGAVEI: [*Rises in a dignified manner*] My name is Dragavei.

VLAD: From now on your name's Layabout.

DRAGAVEI: [*On his knees*] Don't give me such a name.

VLAD: So you don't want me for a Godfather and to christen you.

DRAGAVEI: [*Rising*] Oh well . . . that's different. You can even give the bride away!

VLAD: In this country it's me who christens people and cuts . . . umbilical cords . . .

DRAGAVEI: Well, that's different. My name is Layabout! It suits! But please, I don't want to be an astronomer anymore. Even if you didn't punish me and I went on doing the same work, as soon as the country started to . . .

VLAD: [*Tapping him on the shoulder*] Take your men, Mierlusca too and go to the Danube. Make them climb the trees and leave the sky to itself for a while. Watch the earth instead, look at the ground beyond the waters of the Danube. Tell them to report each day what they've seen. Then mount your horses and return full speed to a place called Poienari and take over the Citadel.

DRAGAVEI: I know the place but it's in ruins.

VLAD: My orders are to take charge of the Citadel.

DRAGAVEI: You want us to make it a stronghold. All right we will. And then . . .

VLAD: We'll defend it.

DRAGAVEI: Against whom?

VLAD: Don't worry. We'll find someone. Now go.

DRAGAVEI: God be praised.

VLAD: What for?

DRAGAVEI: For the phenomenon . . .

Bows and starts to go

VLAD: What's your name?

DRAGAVEI: I'm Private Layabout. From now on, I'm Private Layabout. [*He exits*]

Scene 4

VLAD: He seems a decent enough man. And he made me laugh.

PAPUC: Please, Your Highness, don't tell his father. I promised him. I promised. He's old and wants his son protected.

VLAD: How old is the old fellow?

PAPUC: About eighty. He's a sort of uncle of mine.

VLAD: All right. We'll impale him tomorrow, but I'll keep your promise. I wouldn't tell him for the world. [*Papuc is silent*] Tonight we must also send an envoy to Matthew, King of Hungary. Our kinsmen and friend! And also one to Suceava. Have we any reliable people?

PAPUC: You've put the fear of God into all of them. I don't know whether or not they can be trusted. Can we make them love us if we're always putting the fear of God in them?

VLAD: It's possible.

PAPUC: Then we do have reliable people. Stephen of Moldavia seems pretty safe on his throne.

VLAD: Has he already forgotten that we helped him mount that throne?

PAPUC: No, not at the moment. He keeps sending us tokens of friendship.

VLAD: A good thing . . . friends. Inside the country and abroad. Besides, Stephen and I have always thought alike ever since we were children playing at war. How time flies! And yet thoughts remain the same.

Enter TENEA

Scene 5

TENEA: In this country there's no shame in hanging anyone. We're accountable to no one. Now why is that?

VLAD: I fight for absolute justice. While man, by his very nature, can never be just. He is begotten in sin.

TENEA: Greenish leaf of furze and heather.

Times were bad and they're no better.

Do you know that rhyme?

VLAD: [*Laughing*] It might be that some ill-wishers of mine wrote it for me. I knew I'd never become popular, for man's used to having good things forced on him. Yet when you try to do him good by force he says . . .

TENEA: . . . that you forced him.

VLAD: That's right! He can't see the good. He only notices the force. Yes, that's it.

TENEA: [*Hands him a sheet of paper*] Here are the pretenders. Those who would steal thrones.

VLAD: [*Annoyed*] Why is it always late at night that you show me those who'd take the throne from me?

TENEA: Those were your orders! The black list . . . at midnight.

VLAD: [*Glancing at it*] Look. Thirteen again. This time last year there were only eleven.

TENEA: It fluctuates.

VLAD: [*Looking down the list in amazement*] Gheorge Papuc? On this list?

TENEA: That's what came out of the latest denunciations. Of course, there's no proof yet, that's why I've written PAPUC in large letters and Gheorge in small ones.

VLAD: [*Tears up the paper*] Get out of my sight. Villain! [*Exit* TENEA]

Scene 6

VLAD: I'm tired of all this.

Enter PAPUC:

PAPUC: Did Your Highness call?

VLAD: [*Starting up*] No, nothing . . . except . . . to say I'm tired of everything. Today, I walked about disguised as a tradesman.

PAPUC: Nobody could have recognised you, but you were lucky nothing happened.

VLAD: Those beggars demanding alms have left me covered in scratches. I tossed them coins and the whole town jostled and pushed each other to get at them. They're all after something for nothing. There's not one who wants to do an honest day's work. Why are there so many beggars?

PAPUC: Epidemics . . . battles . . .

VLAD: By the end they'd stolen my purse.

PAPUC: [*Laughing*] That's what I really call slight of hand.

VLAD: It was a keepsake from Mother! Go and get it back for me. [*Indignantly*] Dead dogs on the road side and it doesn't seem to occur to anyone to bury them. Children covered in scabs throwing sand over their heads and fighting like dogs over bones.

PAPUC: Hard times.

VLAD: Who is responsible for them?

PAPUC: We are. But then that's how we found the country. I don't think it's possible to get things right.

VLAD: Can we sit back, arms folded and do nothing?

PAPUC: I don't know . . . perhaps we should.

VLAD: I asked a tradesman what he thought of the new ruling prince . . .

PAPUC: And . . . ?

VLAD: [*Disgusted*] And all he replied was, 'That son of a bitch!' He went on to say that no one could trade honestly in Wallachia because there were so many thieves, that the prince knew of it and did nothing. And he was right. I've turned a blind eye as long as I can. A madman pestered me for a coin to buy some nougat. [*Horrified*] After he'd eaten it, he said he was the prince and had great plans. First, he said, he'd send all those who were against him to hell, impale anyone around him and so rid himself of the lot. He'd sweep the country clean . . . make it shine . . . so shiny you'd slip on the polish. Then he'd lure Mohammed and his army into the country . . . for its clean now . . . chop off Mohammed's head and send his army packing into Poland or even as far as France, and let them fend for themselves. But we'd have to lure as many as possible . . . send them away as long as the road's slippery enough. [*Laughing*] And in the end he didn't eat the nougat, and my purse had gone. He said we should all learn Turkish so that we could imitate them. And then when Mohammed says 'I want to conquer Wallachia' we'd be able to jabber something in Turkish just to confuse them for a year or two.

PAPUC: What more do you expect from a lunatic?

VLAD: No, I'm sure he knows something. His eyes were so bright I felt inclined to place him on the throne and eat the nougat myself (perhaps he'd achieve something).

PAPUC: [*Evasively*] Well . . .

VLAD: [*Thoughtfully looking out of the window*] Stars with tails and officials without heads [*Sighing. To Papuc*] Let's get to work.

ACT
THREE

At Noon

PART ONE

Scene 1

A table is laid out in a church. Beggars are seated on both sides, drinking heavily.

CRIPPLE: [*Angrily*] What do you think you're doing, pouring wine into my ear, you fool! God! Not being able to use your own hands!

BLIND MAN: If you want a blind man to feed you, you've just got to put up with me groping about. I can't find your mouth that easily. Now I've lost my stick . . .

CRIPPLE: Give me a drink.

BLIND MAN: Can't you hear me? I've lost my stick. How can I see without it? And you're always moving around. [*Finds the cripple's mouth with the aid of his stick*].

CRIPPLE: Go on, pour now. You can't miss. [*Opens his mouth wide*] Hey . . .

BLIND MAN: [*Finding an ear instead*] Drink . . .

CRIPPLE: You stupid idiot. You've poured it right into my brain. Any minute now I'll go blind drunk. Damn this feast of charity. I'll be drunk before I've ever tasted anything.

His companions laugh at the sight of them

STAMMERER: He can see . . . I bet he can see. Don't be so mean, blind man. Stop your cheating!

BLIND MAN: To hell with the lot of you! [*Puts down the empty wine jar*] It'll be me that goes without [*Starts eating*] Who'se pinched me victuals?

LAME MAN: Here, take this! [*Gives him a chunk of roast mutton*] Roast mutton. There's plenty for all. Don't you worry, when the Prince gives out food to the poor, he does it in style.

TWISTED-MOUTH: [*Trying to make a speech*] He'll not make a fool of himself. The Prince has gathered all us paupers here, and I reckoned he said to himself, 'If I fill their bellies, my sins'll be forgiven.' Though he's no sinner. He's kind-hearted, he is. Now what sins could God absolve him from? Look how kind he is to us.

STAMMERER: Once in a while, when two Sundays come together.

TWISTED-MOUTH: Well, it suits me. Long live . . .

CRIPPLE: Why is it that this cripple here walks on two stumps?

HUNCHED-BACK WOMAN: Why?

CRIPPLE: So he can look up women's skirts! [*Laughter*]

SCABBY: He knows a lot 'cos he's seen a lot! [*Laughter*]

LAME MAN: You can laugh. If I was you, I'd feel your heads and make sure they're still on your shoulders. There was a boyar in our village who had his head chopped off; someone told on him and when they came to chop it off . . .

CRIPPLE: . . . chop what off?

LAME MAN: When they came to chop off his head. The boyar said to the executioner, 'Look man, you've been my servant too, so I've got one favour to ask you. Grind that sword till it's really sharp.' 'Yes, Sir, of course I will,' he said, 'You've known me since I was a baby. You held me in your arms!' So he went and sharpened his sword and when he came back the boyar asked him, 'Have you sharpened it well?' 'Keen as a razor,' he said. So this boyar laid his head on the block and waits and waits. For about half an hour. Then he gets a bit mad and says, 'What are you waiting for? Can't you cut it off, then?' Whereupon he says, 'I struck it off a long time ago. Just try shaking your head a little!'

FRIGHTENED VOICES: Good God.

SCABBY: [*Off-hand*] Is that all?

LAME MAN: That was all. Now you try shaking your head a little!

SCABBY: Well I never! [*Walks about shaking his head*]

BLIND MAN: Stop all your rubbish. Anyone'd think it were a funeral not a feast.

STAMMERER: Let's make merry now and hope we'll all feel like this when the worst happens, just like today. [*They drink and clink glasses*]

BLIND MAN: The Prince has paid you to be his image maker! He's hit on the right man there [*Choking with laughter*] A mouth of gold.

TWISTED-MOUTH: [*Rhetorically*] Who else gathers the poor all together to give them food? Eh, who else?

SCABBY: You're right. The Prince wants all the paupers on his side.

TWISTED-MOUTH: He's a clever man and sharp.

CRIPPLE: Very clever and sharp as a knife.

LAME MAN: [*Afraid and makes as if to run away*] A knife? Where?

CRIPPLE: Very clever, cripple. About to run off, were you?

BLIND MAN: He'd have gone a long way! [*Laughter*]

LAME MAN: Well . . . I smell a rat [*Entreatingly*] Won't anyone carry me out of here?

BLIND MAN: Take to your heels if you're able.

LAME MAN: Now think . . . think of the money . . . all of us, us dogs. [*Entreatingly*] Someone carry me out of here!

STAMMERER: We've been so busy jawing, my mutton's gone cold. [*Starts to gnaw it*]

CRIPPLE: [*To Blind Man*] Come on, pour, blind man. [*Opens his mouth*]

The PRINCE *enters accompanied by* PAPUC *and a few soldiers*

SOLDIER: His Highness, the Prince.

ALL: [*Amazed*] The Prince!

VLAD: Eat well, paupers!

PAUPERS: [*With mouths full*] Thank you, Your Highness.

VLAD: Is the food good and tasty?

PAUPERS: Like food from the gods, Your Highness.

VLAD: Don't stop eating. Go on, have more. We can talk while you're eating.

LAME MAN: We're afraid of being sick if we eat too much, Your Highness [*Laughs*]

VLAD: [*Smiling*] Eat your fill, good people. I said to myself, 'Perhaps they're hungry.'

CRIPPLE: Well, it were high time for dinner . . . after so many years.

LAME MAN: Our bellies were rumbling.

VLAD: I heard bellies rumbling and said to myself, 'I shall stop all this rumbling in the country.'

STAMMERER: We don't like making a noise, but you can still hear it.

LAME MAN: We're poor and needy. We've crawled here from the edge of the town and not one man or woman would take me in their arms.

BLIND MAN: Women today! . . . [*Sniggers*]

HUNCH-BACKED WOMAN: [*To Blind Man*] You stop sniggering at women! [*They quarrel*]

VLAD: Cease quarrelling! Hunch-back. Can't you forgive?

BLIND MAN: She's got a hump in her head as well! Filled with wickedness, it is. I could never . . . with her . . .

LAME MAN: I crawled through on all fours through ditches and muddy roads to get here and beg from Your Highness.

STAMMERER: Wretched people that we are!

VLAD: [*To Papuc*] Captain Papuc, see they have another cask of wine. And a young calf. [*Papuc motions to a young soldier who goes out*]

HUNCH-BACKED WOMAN: Long live Your Highness! You've a heart of gold!

BLIND MAN: It's so pitch black at night I knock into all the fences. [*Afraid*] They don't half stink.

VLAD: They're not fences. They're stakes. Live palings. Did that never occur to you?

BLIND MAN: If it had . . . If Your Highness wants to impale anyone you have the right to do it. I mean, who can stop you? [*Thoughtfully*] I thought they were posts.

VLAD: Stakes, blind man, because thieving is rife.

LAME MAN: [*To Hunch-Backed Woman*] I want to get away . . .

HUNCH-BACKED WOMAN: Why can't you stop fidgeting, you devil. It's as if you've got worms inside you.

CRIPPLE: Somebody nearly robbed me the day before yesterday, but I gave him such a fistful. He was trying to steal my goblets.

VLAD: What goblets? [*Cripple coughs*]

HUNCH-BACKED WOMAN: No one steals nothing now.

BLIND MAN: I mean, who would steal anything now? Perhaps other crimes, Your Highness . . . but as for stealing . . . well, who dares today?

CRIPPLE: [*Feeling self-conscious*] Me.

VLAD: You're boasting. Where do you live?

CRIPPLE: In the haberdashers' district, past the tanners.

VLAD: Did you drink cold water at the pump today?

CRIPPLE: Yes . . . I did.

VLAD: Did you see a fine goblet?

CRIPPLE: I did.

VLAD: I placed it there on purpose. Just to see how men behave. . .

CRIPPLE: [*Takes out two goblets he has hidden inside his shirt*] And here they are, Your Highness.

VLAD: What about them?

CRIPPLE: The goblets . . . I took 'em . . . I just tried to . . . I stole one . . . and then the next day there was another, just like this one.

VLAD: And who put it there?

CRIPPLE: People. Others. They knew that if it weren't found, the whole lot of us would have to go to prison.

VLAD: [*Admiringly*] You charlatan!

CRIPPLE: So in the end I took 'em both and I would have stolen the third they put out but the feast was announced and there weren't time.

VLAD: I was considering cutting off your other hand as well.

CRIPPLE: Oh I shouldn't do that. I'd only steal with my feet.

VLAD: As you confessed it yourself, we'll pardon you.

CRIPPLE: I didn't steal 'em out of wickedness, Your Highness. I just wanted to see if I could do it. The harder it is the faster I can steal. It . . .

VLAD: [*To Papuc*] Fill these goblets with wine. I want to drink the health of the last thief left in the land.

PAPUC: [*Pouring the wine*] It's not been washed out, Your Highness.

A cask of wine is brought into the church, along with trays of steaks and chunks of roast meat.

VLAD: [*Drinking*] Cripple, your health! You're lucky I'm in a good mood.

CRIPPLE: I know the best time to confess.

THE OTHERS: [*Raising their cups*] May God give us peace, Your Highness, for us here in the country can all get on with each other.

CRIPPLE: The leper loves you because you're cruel. It's getting harder and harder to steal because you punish so severely.

VLAD: [*Raising the goblet to the others*] You've met with hard times in my reign, thieves. [*Laughter*]

BEGGERS: [*Raising their cups*] Long live Your Highness . . . so we'll have plenty of time to rid us of our nasty ways.

HUNCH-BACKED WOMAN: I'll mend mine when two Sundays run next to each other.

VLAD: I thought we could get together and see what could be done.

BLIND MAN: What is to be done? You won't let us steal or tell lies. You can't beg – for no one's got anything to give. You can't

65

speak ill of people for there's no one left to talk to. Everyone avoids each other. You can't even scratch yourself, or they cut off your hands. It's a sorry tale!

STAMMERER: Our own people won't have anything to do with us.

HUNCH-BACKED WOMAN: We've come down to beggary.

STAMMERER: We sleep out in the open, anywhere will do. Under some eaves, bridges or makeshift ones.

VLAD: [*Affectionately*] Do you think I might be able to stop such suffering?

BEGGARS: Oh yes, Your Highness, if you had a mind to.

VLAD: Yes, perhaps I could . . . if I had a mind to . . .

BLIND MAN: But if not even Your Highness is on the side of the blind.

LAME MAN: The lame . . .

HUNCH-BACKED WOMAN: The hunch-backed . . .

SCABBY: . . . With the . . .

LEPER: Lepers.

TWISTED-MOUTH: – Those with the twisted mouths . . .

VLAD: [*Furiously*] Stop! That will do! I side with all riff-raff.

BEGGARS: Long live the Prince for he sides with all riff-raff.

VLAD: [*Contented*] I won't have you flattering me, thieves!

BEGGARS: Your health! [*Laughter*]

VLAD: Rogues! Swindlers!

BEGGARS: To His Highness [*Raising their cups*]

VLAD: Cut-throats!

BEGGARS: Hooray!

VLAD: Villains! Fools!

BEGGARS: Hurray!

VLAD: Scum of the earth! I've brought you here to keep you together.

BEGGARS: Ha, ha, ha! That's kind of you, Your Highness. The milk of human kindness, he is!

VLAD: Can I rely on you?

BLIND MAN: He's a force to be reckoned with.

CRIPPLE: You can't imagine the hunger of all of us put together.

VLAD: I'm not going to let you loaf about any more, filling the taverns and sleeping under bridges. You'll not be a burden to anyone ever again, or stand in anyone's way.

BEGGARS: Long live Your Highness. A blessing, you are, a God – send!

Enter a soldier

Scene 2

SOLDIER: [*In a low voice to the Prince*] The rest are here.

VLAD: Is there room for them all in here?

SOLDIER: A few too many. Still, if we pack them into the church as well, and they're very eager. Say it's three years since . . . Now's the time for us to . . .

VLAD: Have they brought their ledgers with them?

SOLDIER: Oh yes. All in good order, tributes, interests, etc.

VLAD: [*Aloud and solemnly*] The Turks!

BEGGARS: Oh hell! Christ save us!

LAME MAN: But we can't fight, Your Highness. We'll never resist them. There are too many of them. We'd better try and humour them.

VLAD: That sounds a good idea. You try it, for I've been trying to do just that for the last three years and they've lost their patience.

Enter the Turkish envoys. They bow low. Dead silence

Scene 3

VLAD: You are welcome on the hospitable soil of Wallachia.

SULEIMAN: We have always felt at home here. You have welcomed us with music and drums. But the almighty and just, merciful Sultan is angry with you, Highness. He says, 'May your end be a happy one.'

VLAD: And what exactly does he mean by that?

SULEIMAN: To die on your throne.

VLAD: We shall see.

SULEIMAN: He says on account of the fact that you lack energy in serving us . . .

VLAD: That's not possible. He must be mistaken. Perhaps he's mistaken me for someone else.

SULEIMAN: . . . and because there have been some delays in fulfilling his orders.

THE AGA: [*Counting on his fingers*] The war minister . . . coach horses . . . the palace gateman . . . the leader of the soldiers . . .

VLAD: What delays were there? [*To the Aga*] And what horses are you talking about, man? [*To the beggars*] Be quiet!

BEGGARS: [*Looking at each other*] Perhaps they'll get rid of him. [*They gather in a circle round the Prince and start to move around erratically, mocking him and shouting*] You'll lose your throne, you'll be dethroned . . .

VLAD: [*Gently*] Children be quiet!

BEGGARS: [*The same as before*] It's your own fault. You'll lose your throne, na, na, na, na, na, na, na . . .

VLAD: [*Trying to control himself*] I'll drive the lot of you out of here! [*To the soldier*] Where is the captain of the guards?

SOLDIER: Somewhere around.

VLAD: [*To the beggars*] Calm down!

The beggars become quieter

SULEIMAN: Our almighty, just and merciful Sultan is still hoping you will pay the tribute and send gifts to the Porte.

AGA: He says, 'Was it for this we put him on the throne? For this we wined and dined him so well?'

VLAD: The food was good, I grant you, but the royal kaftan's started to come apart at the seams. If I ever catch sight of that tailor again . . .

AGA: He says, 'Was it for this we gave him the green banner and a badge of office?'

SULEIMAN: So he sent us both here to remind you . . .

VLAD: So, that's why you've come? Do you want to 'do your business' right here in my closet?

SULEIMAN: Yes indeed, so long as Your Highness's gold ingots are there! And the children we're owed and the falcons!

VLAD: [*To Papuc*] Put down falcons. Don't forget or we'll never live it down. [*To the envoys*] Of course. Why not? They're well trained with wings spread . . .

SULEIMAN: And it is very important that we travel with soldiers. We need a brave captain to escort us and the Sultan's gifts in safety to the Danube.

VLAD: What do you say to that, Aga Carasol? [*Pointing to Suleiman*] Don't you think our friend here is overdoing it a bit? Isn't it rather a large tribute? Perhaps he'd like us to give him bison and deer as well. All you have to do is ask. If the request is carefully worded, Romanian supplies are as good as delivered.

AGA: You have no idea how angry the Sultan is! He remembered that he'd seen you in Istanbul wearing yellow boots and a green coat made of satin. Things that foreigners never wear.

VLAD: [*To Papuc*] I've never worn yellow boots in my life. He's mistaken me for someone else again. [*To the envoys*] I have great respect for the merciful Mohammed and I am deeply sorry that he has such a distorted opinion of me. I should very much like to distort it a little in the opposite direction so as to even things out a bit . . . bring some normality to the situation.

SULEIMAN: Give him what he demands.

BLIND MAN: Woe is me. Woe to all of us. If they come to an agreement we'll all be beggared and there really will be no one left to beg from.

CRIPPLE: Ah don't worry. They'll never come to an agreement.

SULEIMAN: Brothers for eternity.

BLIND MAN: Eternity, my arse! Listen how they flatter each other.

CRIPPLE: [*Whispering to the Blind Man*] How can you believe all that. Can't you tell, it's a load of codswallop?

VLAD: Tell me, honourable guests, envoys of the mighty Mohammed, our father and pillar, what wind brings you here to this country? Oh, I forgot, you've already told me. Now for the ledgers. Are they all totalled and multiplied?

SULEIMAN: Yes, including interest. [*To Aga*] Read the vizier's report.

AGA: [*Opening the ledger*] The tribute for the year 1456 . . . one hundred bags of gold coins.

LAME MAN: Oh the food and drink such money would buy!

AGA: For the year . . . three hundred bags . . . because we have tripled the tribute, it not being paid when doubled!

HUNCH-BACKED WOMAN: They're fleecing us. Skinning us alive, the villains.

AGA: And five hundred bags for the present year and besides that – one thousand children to be brought up in Istanbul as Janissaries for the Sultan.

VLAD: And besides that . . . you were saying?

AGA: To finish – slaves to sweep all the chimneys in Istanbul.

VLAD: [*To Suleiman*] And is it you who's going to take these back to the Sultan?

SULEIMAN: Yes, we must. Otherwise he will fly into a rage. And it's not pleasant when he gets angry [*Confidentially*] You know, Your Highness, there are many string-pullers and schemers who are forever pouring ideas into his head.

VLAD: What do you expect me to do about it?

SULEIMAN: He is mad with rage.

VLAD: Who?

AGA: The Sultan. You must pay on the nail. That's what he said.

VLAD: I can only give you the children right now.

SULEIMAN: Which children?

VLAD: [*Pointing to the beggars*] These. They're a bit ricketty. We've had a few hard years due to the weather. We've had to tighten our belts . . . and things are a little difficult at the moment. We had thought . . . he'd exempt us!

SULEIMAN: Exempt you, Your Highness?

VLAD: That's right, exempt us.

BLIND MAN: [*To Twisted-mouth*] Listen to that Twisted-mouth. Can't you shout out something. You can see he's cornered. He needs help!

STAMMERER: Make the bloody creep change sides. [*Aloud*] Long live our cousin the Impaler.

TWISTED-MOUTH: Great! [*Coughs*] Honourable Tartars!

BLIND MAN: Turks.

TWISTED-MOUTH: Honourable carters . . . the tribute is sacred to us. We know we should have paid by now, but our only thought has been to try to save as much as we could, even to give you the shirts off our backs, our goats, our children. Who else would give you things if we didn't?

BLIND MAN: What a speaker!

TWISTED-MOUTH: Trust us! Go on, back to your country and we'll send the tribute. No doubt it'll get there before you do.

> Cut it short, set off on your tracks.
> For a groat you'll take the shirt off our backs.

SULEIMAN: We're not leaving here until you pay us all you owe . . . in cash.

TWISTED-MOUTH: In cash? We'll pay it all in one go! We'll shovel it out. Empty the whole muck heap of a closet . . . I mean . . . treasury . . . in bucketfuls if necessary.

VLAD: [*To Twisted-mouth*] Stop interfering, friend. [*To Suleiman*] In our opinion . . .

HUNCH-BACKED WOMAN [*To Cripple*] The Prince has made fun of us long enough.

CRIPPLE: [*Shocked*] Fun of the people! That's a dirty trick to play on humble people!

HUNCH-BACKED WOMAN: Let's side with the Turks. I bet they're more powerful.

One potato, two potato,
On the beat, take your seat.

CRIPPLE: That's right. They also brought someone with them to bargain with us. Pit-a-pat-bang!

A GROUP: [*To Vlad*] What have you done with the water that once was in Wallachia? Why this drought, eh? Why is there no rain? It's because of them. That's why!

VLAD: [*To Suleiman, resuming his conversation unperturbed*] As I was saying . . . we'll give you as much as we can now and the rest . . . later.

BEGGARS: Hear! Hear!

VLAD: I can't humiliate a whole country . . .

SULEIMAN: I can't hear what you're saying.

VLAD: [*Pointing to the beggars*] They have the right to speak their minds.

BEGGARS: Hear! Hear!

SULEIMAN: With us the situation's tenser.

VLAD: So they will learn a lot then.

SULEIMAN: From whom?

VLAD: From all of you. I suggest you accept these instead of the children.

SULEIMAN: [*Quite surprised*] This scum?

VLAD: Innocent babes.

SULEIMAN: These . . . tottering wretches?

BEGGARS: Listen to that!

VLAD: Suckling babes. Crying out for succour.

LAME MAN: Your Highness. Can I go and have a pee? [*Makes as if to go out*]

VLAD: Stay where you are, cripple. You can wait.

LAME MAN: I came here to eat not starve.

VLAD: To have your fill. You'll have your fill. [*To Suleiman*] Think it over beshli-aghasi. Was that right?

SULEIMAN: [*Offended*] You're laughing at me. [*Laughing*] Well, it's not a bad joke!

VLAD: That's how we are. Suddenly we feel like joking. Ha, ha, ha!

They all roar with laughter, beggars, and Turks alike. Meanwhile, Vlad, Papuc and the soldiers steal out of the church. A soldier returns to summon Aga towards him. Aga follows him out.

SULEIMAN: How cheerful they all are!

LEPER: We say what we think. Speak our minds . . . ha, ha, ha!

71

SULEIMAN: It's a treat for me to come for tribute to Wallachia. I haven't had such a good laugh for years.

CRIPPLE: Our prince often jests.

BLIND MAN: The idea. Fancy offering us as tribute! [*Laughter*]

CRIPPLE: It'd be good for us to go and see their Empire.

BLIND MAN: Here Turk, where are you? Take us with you to see your country. [*Gropes for him with his stick*]

ALL: [*Entreatingly*] Take us with you, Turk, Take us . . .

BLIND MAN: Hey you. Damn you and your tribute. Go and hang yourself.

HUNCH-BACKED WOMAN: [*Afraid*] Fire!

CRIPPLE: That's how it is. You can't teach your grandfather to suck eggs!

HUNCH-BACKED WOMAN: Fire!

CRIPPLE: We know how clever you are!

BLIND MAN: Fire! I sense the smell!

LEPER: A child once burnt fears fire.

The stage fills with smoke. Shrieks are heard. They all rush to the door.

VOICES: Move! Move! Get out of the way!

CRIPPLE: It's locked. They've locked us in!

Shrieks. They rush to the windows. One drops his crutches and starts running and shouting.

SULEIMAN: Move out of the way. The Sultan's expecting me! [*He rushes to the door, the windows, and then starts hammering on the walls with his bare fists*]

VOICES: We'll be burnt alive. Oh God! Help!

LEPER: No! You're crushing me. My belly! Oh!

SULEIMAN: Allah! Where are you, Aga? Allah! Aga! Go tell the prince I'll depose him. I'll send him under guard to . . .

BLIND MAN: We're done for, brothers. The ceiling's cracking!

SULEIMAN: I am the personal envoy of the Sultan. He has sent me here to find out how things stand and report back.

HUNCH-BACKED WOMAN: Shut up, you! Bird of ill-omen!

SULEIMAN: I'll have you all as slaves!

VOICES: Get him!

General uproar. Smoke

PART TWO

Scene 1

DOMNICA *and* MARIȚA *in Domnica's bedchamber*

DOMNICA: No. He comes from a good family . . . with a three storeyed house in Padua and a sailing ship in the port of Venice. To say nothing of boats, olive groves in Fiesole and . . .

MARIȚA: Have you seen all this for yourself?

DOMNICA: No, he told me about it. I didn't see why I shouldn't believe him!

MARIȚA: Hmm! He's got you on the end of a string! Do you really believe all that? You're still a child, a fledgeling.

DOMNICA: He can see the Pope whenever he wants to Mariţa. No one ever stops him. On his father's side . . . he's descended from the kings of France . . . and on his mother's side . . .

MARIȚA: [*Spitefully*] When has he had time to fill your ears with all this nonsense?

DOMNICA: On Sundays . . . at church. [*Laughs*] I don't know how he manages it but he's always next to me. He keeps whispering on and on and on, and all I do is listen.

MARIȚA: What a way to carry on!

DOMNICA: He calls me 'Lady straight-laced' because I'm always straight in everything I do. And he calls me a saint, just as if I were a piece of sacred wood . . . A nice piece of stuff to work on. That's what he said. Every night he comes to my door and crosses himself just as if he's worshipping. Time and again I've saved him from the executioners. They swore he was a thief.

MARIȚA: [*Furiously*] You shouldn't encourage him. The wretch. Never go to the neighbouring village to choose a husband. Even less a total stranger. It's the likes of him who'd seduce you, then leave you stranded on some foreign shore.

DOMNICA: Oh! Heaven forbid!

73

MARIŢA: That comes from being an orphan: You believe anything. Your parents, God rest their souls, were killed by the heathens. When will you ever learn? There used to be a girl here . . . who eloped with some Persian envoy. First he courted her, gave her gifts . . . a ring, a scarf. Then stole a kiss, and finally got what he was after, and when she went to Persia, she found he'd already got five wives.

DOMNICA: Good Lord!

MARIŢA: The same will happen to you, my girl.

DOMNICA: Everyone worries as if they cared!

MARIŢA: That's why I'm here. I've brought you some sorrel. Boil it, let it simmer a bit, then drink it down and you'll soon get your appetite back again. Can't you see, you're as thin as a rake? Men like strong women, plump and healthy, nicely filled out a bit . . . swaying hips . . . you know. They don't like them thin as a board, only good to iron their breeches on.

DOMNICA: I don't want an appetite. I wish I was dead. [*Starts to cry*]

MARIŢA: You're just a child, love. Ah, before I forget, your lover's at the door!

DOMNICA: Tell him to go away!

MARIŢA: Oh, all right then. [*Exits*]

PAINTER: [*Enters, holding a box in one hand and a drawing in the other*] The gentle lady informed me I may enter.

DOMNICA: I don't believe you! [*Trying to be dignified and hold back her tears*] I gave her quite different orders.

PAINTER: [*Puzzled*] She said you were not engaged. . .

DOMNICA: Well my heart . . . is.

PAINTER: [*Emphatically*] What? Have the Turks got that far? When I next see my cousin . . . Baudouin of Flanders . . . I shall say, 'Have you need of a soldier. One determined to fight single-handed against a hundred saracens? Here is one for you to command!'

DOMNICA: You never stop talking.

PAINTER: [*Showing her the drawing*] That's what a door looks like, here today. I have painted the door of your bedchamber so many times! And here I am wasting my time like a servant waiting on a young lady of Tîrgovişte. I who enter palaces of royalty. Oh how ridiculous I feel!

DOMNICA: You're not far off it!

PAINTER: Oh dear! I quite forgot this box I'm carrying. Pandora's box . . . I have here a small gift just for you! [*Drops the box. It opens, revealing a single shoe*]

DOMNICA: Whatever next! A single shoe . . . and for my right foot only. The other day you left a stocking, yesterday a glove. Your gifts are nothing but a heap of odds and ends, never a pair . . . and he says he loves me! That set of glasses you brought isn't complete either. Every time you come you bring a single glass.

PAINTER: [*Turning pale*] Giuseppe, that mascalzone!

DOMNICA: Who? Your footman?

PAINTER: Yes. It is he who rummages in the boxes. Divides the sets. It never occurred to me to examine the boxes to see if they were complete. I'll see he gets his true deserts!

DOMNICA: Well, that's your affair! Give him these as well. [*Goes to the adjoining room and comes back with her arms full of odd objects*] Here, take them! Then he'll be able to pair them off. And now please go. I have a violent headache.

PAINTER: A Sunday headache . . . It's the fashion nowadays: headaches on Sundays because then our rhythms are all upset. We rise late, lie a-bed longer . . . we . . .

DOMNICA: Oh, I have headaches on other days too . . . Saturdays, Fridays, Thursdays . . .

PAINTER: Why didn't you tell me before? I could have asked for some medicine from Padua. There's an apothecary there who . . .

DOMNICA: No, no! Thank you [*Shouting*] . . . Mariţa. Please. . .

MARIŢA: [*Entering*] I was having a bit of a rest and then just happened to be passing . . .

DOMNICA: I knew you'd be around somewhere! Please help this gentleman carry his things back to his lodgings. [*Mariţa takes them all in her arms*] And be careful not to drop anything on the way. Giuseppe needs them . . . badly!

PAINTER: I'll pack them at once. [*Exits*]

DOMNICA: [*Alone now*] I had to make him understand . . . once and for all. Some gentleman! Riding his high horse, pretending he's of noble birth. His sailing ships stagnating in some port or another, and yet he can't afford to buy me one pair of anything.

PART THREE

Scene 1

In the churchyard, some distance from the place of the dreadful fire. Muffled groans are heard.

VLAD: [*Walks about irritated. From time to time he stops, examines a cross, then raises his fist threateningly in the direction of the noise*] What have you got against me? What do you want? Why the persecution?

Scene 2

VLAD: Is there a beehive round here? There's a lot of humming! I can't even hear my own thoughts!

PAPUC: [*Goes upstage and shouts out loudly*] Silence! Shut your mouths! His Highness is planning the future of the country and can't hear his own thoughts. [*The humming stops for a while. Silence, then from within, a voice, 'Who's playing with fire?'*] [*Papuc shouts again*] Shut up! [*Coming back to the Prince*] There's peace in the country now.

VLAD: What did they want?

PAPUC: Well, you know how it is. They're frightened. Want to get out.

VLAD: Let them piss the fire out. Pity about the church!

PAPUC: We'll build another.

VLAD: Quite. Order it done tomorrow . . . or rather the day after tomorrow. We'll let the earth breathe a little first, shall we? Then we'll build on the same spot, a church dedicated to the Assumption. Then, a few quick devotions and we'll make the heavens throb with fervour . . .

PAPUC: What do you intend to do with the Turk, Sir?

VLAD: Which one? Ah yes, bring him here. [*Papuc goes out and returns immediately, accompanied by the Aga who is terrified. His hands are bound*]

Scene 3

VLAD: Why are you trembling – shaking all over . . . honourable Aga?

AGA: I . . . tremble with cold.

VLAD: Captain, warm him a little. [*Papuc drags him nearer the fire*]

AGA: Allah! Allah!

VLAD: Winter will soon be here, honourable guest, and the dreadful weather around here has affected you. [*To Papuc*] Release him! Untie his hands. [*Papuc does so rather unwillingly*] You are free, Aga!

AGA: [*Afraid*] Me . . . Free?

VLAD: Yes, you are free. Don't you know what freedom means? Have you never tasted it before? You can go home!

AGA: Home! Where?

VLAD: And tell those who sent you exactly what you've seen.

AGA: [*Unable to recover his senses*] What I've seen?

VLAD: [*To Papuc*] This man's not in his right mind. I hope you didn't beat him up. Such shame there'd be! [*To Aga*] Did they hit you about the head? [*Aga shakes his head*] Go and tell the Sultan that we do not hit out with fists. [*Turning on him*] Out of my sight! If you don't run to Istanbul as fast as your legs will carry you, we'll run this sword right through your body.

AGA: [*Falls to his knees*] Oh, thank you.

VLAD: What! Still here? [*Aga rises and takes to his heels*] Tell the Sultan to keep quiet and be reasonable. We should have set one of the beggars free. He'd have gone from pillar to post telling everyone what happens to beggars. Go, quickly! [*Papuc is about to run and then*] Oh, these Captains of mine are useless. They never shift themselves. They leave it all to me.

PAPUC: It's rather late. The dogs have already taken over . . .

VLAD: I have to see to everything.

PAPUC: Well, as it happens, one did escape. I didn't dare to tell you beforehand.

VLAD: One of ours?

PAPUC: Yes. What you'd call the original Pauper. The Lame Man. God knows how he managed to get away. Perhaps through the legs of the men locking the doors.

VLAD: [*Disappointed*] It'll be Doomsday before that tortoise crawls the length and breadth of Wallachia and I intend to tidy things up among my subjects well before then. What happens above is nothing compared to what's going on down here. Right now! Go, see to the army! There'll be others here soon enough asking for tribute.

PAPUC: Your Highness's soldiers are ready, armed to the teeth.

VLAD: Well, tell them that whatever happens they are to avoid eating their swords. No matter how loud their bellies rumble. [*Papuc is about to go*] And don't forget to call on the bishop. Tell him not to forget about the consecration of the church and to ask God to forgive us immediately. Oh, and wait! [*Papuc comes back*] Where is Rozmalin?

PAPUC: He has left with part of the army to face Dan Basarab who is marching against us with help from the people of Braşov. [*Laugh*]

VLAD: What if he betrays us?

PAPUC: What, my best friend and your most faithful servant? Impossible!

Scene 4

VLAD: I've tapped the cask . . . that is . . . the situation. The Turks will pour in like torrents, and many other things. Heads will roll too. Hold your ground, man! [*Smiling*] Some call me the Impaler behind my back, but I impale them quite openly. Anyway, I've managed to create a name for myself. Short! Expressive! And easy to remember. [*Looking at the palm of his hand*] My life-line itches. [*Kneels and touches the ground with his open palm upwards*] This country's life-line now passes through this pile of dust in my hand. Lord, don't cut off the life-line of this handful of earth. All our toiling and suffering is only for. . .

Enter TENEA *and* PAPUC

Scene 5

TENEA: [*Annoyed*] My lord . . . [*Points to a bag he is carrying*]
VLAD: What is it?
TENEA: Rozmalin. Dan Basarab caught him, hacked him to pieces and sent him here like this. His horse came alone carrying the bag.
VLAD: Poor man! What about his army?
PAPUC: Routed. A surprise attack. Most of them perished. Dan has so many cannons.
VLAD: So we haven't burnt the candles, church and all that was in it in vain, then? Yes, even the church had to go.
PAPUC: The smoke is starting to choke us. Aren't you afraid?
VLAD: It's lucky I'm not afraid of drowning, for here's what we'll do.

He asks Papuc to come closer and they start talking in whispers

Scene 6

AGA: [*Enters almost in tears*] They won't let me . . .
PAPUC: [*Laughing*] Look who we've saved from the fire, sir! He can't even run away.
AGA: I've tried every direction. They would have struck me with lances or shot arrows at me. One wanted to empty his gun into me.
VLAD: Did you try crossing the Danube. Wasn't that possible?
AGA: I have no papers.
VLAD: What about the mountains?
AGA: Why should I go to the mountains?
VLAD: You could get back to Istanbul via Transylvania. But careful Aga, beware of our men who fire without warning. Then if you get to the Sultan you can give him all the details.
AGA: [*Entreatingly*] Give me a letter . . . a pass . . .
VLAD: I haven't time to write letters. Get out! [*Aga goes*]
PAPUC: He's so helpless!
VLAD: [*Turning on him*] He's brought shame on me . . . [*Smiles*] [*A moment of silence. From the monastery comes the faint sound of voices: 'Who's playing with fire?'*]

79

PART FOUR

Scene 1

A little later in the forest. The two impaled men are talking.

ROMANIAN: There is a man around here who prolongs our lives.
TURK: The devil he does!
ROMANIAN: It's true. He's very good at it.
TURK: The devil he is!
ROMANIAN: All the rich consult him, old men, old hags. I don't know what the medicine is he gives them, but the minute they take it they start to giggle. [*Laughs*]
TURK: That's life!
ROMANIAN: [*An idea dawns*] How about you complaining as well?
TURK: What about? That I've not been impaled quite right!
ROMANIAN: No, not that. Complain you haven't had a trial.
TURK: Oh! [*Sighs*]
ROMANIAN: Dawn's breaking. [*After a pause*] And I'm not broken yet. Man can resist, such is the life within him! Poor life . . . in fact it's almost noon. Noon is breaking, noon . . . I'm raving.

Scene 2

VLAD: [*Enters. He is cheerful*] Hello, lads.
ROMANIAN: You?
VLAD: I see you're holding on.
ROMANIAN: Obviously, since I've croaked.
VLAD: I examined the files. Miscarriage of justice! Executioners! [*Enter the executioners*] You trouble-makers. Oafs! What are you staring it?
PÎRVU: Shall we beat him to a pulp?

VLAD: Is that all you can say? Take him down!

CHIORU: What?

VLAD: If he dies, you will suffer.

ROMANIAN: I'm dying now. Don't let them touch me. Don't shake me or . . .

VLAD: Easy, lad. Courage . . . Bear it a little longer . . . Perhaps you'll be saved. God is mighty!

ROMANIAN: Me? From here? I won't get down. I shan't get down without the Turk. He's my brother. Aren't you, Selim?

VLAD: It'd take a miracle to save you! [*To the executioners*] Sprinkle some water on him. Call the healers to come with their charms. I want him safe and sound and fit to wear his sword by tonight. [*To himself*] It's high time we raised the dead to help us resist. A pity so many are dead in their graves.

PÎRVU: We're not so stupid that we can't raise them again . . . We're sorry we took so much trouble in vain . . . All for nothing . . . [*Laughing*] You can't imagine the effort we put into torturing them all.

VLAD: I'll resuscitate him with my own hands. Breathe life into his body, myself. [*Starts mouth to mouth resuscitation*] My stake thrusts its roots deep into the soul of this country. Sends out shoots. Its branches are your arms. My unseen soldiers. I am cruel and it hurts. You only punish those you love.

Scene 3

Enter PAPUC, *excited. He whispers to* VLAD

VLAD: [*About to go*] Good work!

CHIORU: What about . . . [*Points to the stakes*]

VLAD: Damn. I haven't time now. I'm quite attached to this lad. See to it that you don't hurt him getting him down.

ROMANIAN: Don't let them touch me!

VLAD: Yes . . . you'd better leave him where he is until I return . . . the Turk too. Let him live. Maybe we will pardon him too. [*To the two impaled*] Goodbye . . . villains. [*Exits*]

PART FIVE

Scene 1

The Palace. Domnica's Bedroom

DOMNICA: You've not been here for quite a while. Still suffering?

PAINTER: My heart . . . here. Have you a knife, for I never carry a weapon? The artist's weapon is far more terrible . . . his art. He has no need of a sword or dagger. It would be mere tautology. Why not kill me yourself. Here . . .[*Unbuttons his shirt*]

DOMNICA: Italians! Their gestures are always so pompous. Where did you learn to act like that?

PAINTER: [*Helplessly*] From Giuseppe . . . Yet he was always a success. After such a scene he conquered any woman. She would take him into her arms and beg him not to kill himself. Then he would roar. 'No, I can live no longer. May heaven protect you!' And then goes as if to thrust a dagger through his chest. He was only acting and yet what emotion he suffered! You see he was a Neapolitan, my lady!

DOMNICA: Why don't you try being yourself . . . in love. You, the way nature made you, for better or for worse, but at any rate be yourself. Your real self.

PAINTER: I was my true self . . . until last year, but now I hardly recognize myself anymore, and it's all your fault. It's you who have changed my whole being, my way of life, of love, even my thoughts on art. Why won't you accompany me?

DOMNICA: Where?

PAINTER: You know where . . . Where everything is cared for, stratified, polished, painted, for hundreds of years . . for a millennium. In Rome there are houses left untouched since Nero.

DOMNICA: That madman?

PAINTER: Yes, but in Rome madness passes . . . buildings last. Here the truth is in reverse: Buildings vanish with their generations as though graves for the living, and when the inhabitants die, the graves also sink into the ground and another grave is built for the next generation. Nothing lasts. Things are but leaves that fall from the trees in autumn. If they don't fall of their own volition, they are pulled down by those who govern this land. If they resist, neighbours perform that task, if not the neighbours, thieves, enter their houses to rob them. Never before have I witnessed such deeds. When I first came here I recorded it all, but then discarded the idea. It was always the same five or six disasters to report. I respect the heroism of your Prince . . . a prophet in the wilderness, yet he tries too hard to keep his ground and set things to rights. Here in the midst of the apocalypse. He attempts to put faith into the hearts of his people and the seeds of their future. He rails at God and then repents. He acts without guilt only to repent. Once at a sitting held in the early hours, I shudder now to recall the repentance on his face. He who is most gentle, makes pretence of being cruel merely because he thinks it wise to do so. One should not judge the man by the mask.

DOMNICA: Yes, you've spoken sincerely this time, but too sincerely, for you understand nothing.

PAINTER: Quite the contrary. I understand . . . everything! Not only that which occurs here today, but I could also relate – and know it to be an almost certain truth – events which will take place here tomorrow. Should you wish . . . I will draw it for you . . .

DOMNICA: Another chapter of disasters?

PAINTER: Not quite.

DOMNICA: Then I give up. I like things that are new, not expected.

PAINTER: But wait. First . . . Don't you realize that great pressure has been put upon the Prince just so that he will submit to the Turks, and yet should he do so, he is surely lost. For they will take him to Constantinople and well guarded too. His head will be stuffed full of cotton-wool and stuck on a pole at the gate of the seraglio. And even if they did not take him there, he doesn't stand a chance, and if this year Mohammed fails this campaign he's prepared so carefully, he will only start it again the next or certainly the following year. Who could possibly resist him?

DOMNICA: We'll be all right, women and children as well. Look at me. I'm learning how to use a lasso and I'm commander of a troup of horsemen.

PAINTER: Well, body and soul ties you to the land, but there are not many like you, my lady. And besides I have something far more unpleasant to relate.

DOMNICA: [*Curiously*] What?

PAINTER: Matthew Corvin. Don't count on any help from him whatsoever.

DOMNICA: How can you be so sure?

PAINTER: Let's look dispassionately at these events, the man Corvin has a great deal of interest in strengthening links with the West. He covets the throne of the Emperor at Vienna. He has no need of a war against the Turks. He will not aid Vlad, and besides, were Matthew to catch him – God forbid! – he would imprison him for ten or twelve years at least. And there is more. [*Secretly*] There is one in Braşov who is a German, an expert in the forgery of every kind of letter ever written by the Wallachian Prince. No matter how valiant or brave your Prince is, he's sure to fall, defeated by political intrigue and the pulling of strings.

DOMNICA: Why are you telling me all this?

PAINTER: I am an artist and cannot hold back the truth. I would have warned the Prince myself were it not for the man Tenea who is forever barring my way.

DOMNICA: Watch out for him! His words are so virulent they'd eat away the vessel they were kept in. So what plans do you have for us?

PAINTER: I shall never leave you here, in a place of such unrest. Should you refuse to come of your own accord, I shall take you by force. It happens to be a custom of these parts. The young man goes to the 'hora', seizes the lass of his choice, carries her to his abode and the following day sets out to war to die for his country, cheerfully whistling. And the absurd part is that he dies, and the young girl gives birth to a child.

DOMNICA: [*Laughing*] I'm beginning to like you . . . just a bit. [*Kisses him*]

PAINTER: Wait, where are you going – with only one kiss?

DOMNICA: Yes, just one – one of a pair!

Scene 2

A state room in the palace

PAPUC: I've caught him!
VLAD: Alive?
PAPUC: Alive.
VLAD: Arrogant Dan! It breaks my heart.
PAPUC: The commander of the cavalry, Tenea, has crossed the mountains with a company of soldiers. He'll be back later. But now this Dan is begging for mercy.
VLAD: Mercy? [*Laughs*] My father, the late Vlad Dracula quarrelled with Iancu of Hunedoara who then caught him and chopped off his head. That was after he'd chopped off the head of my younger brother, Mircea, who'd only been on the throne a few months. With the help of this Iancu, I took the throne. I overlooked the fact that he'd been so cruel to my family and was glad to accept such friendly support. In the meantime we began to organise this little country. Dan continually plotted and schemed in Braşov to have my head for the block. And now we've caught him and he has the temerity to ask us not to chop off his head!
PAPUC: In those last few utterances you've mentioned chopping off heads five times. Is that because you lack a richer vocabulary?
VLAD: [*Laughing*] It's only in the last ten years that chopping off heads has gained popularity! It could be that I lack a better vocabulary, but at any rate, there's certainly no lack of princely heads. [*Indignantly*] So, Dan wants me to take pity on him, eh! He only deserves punishment by the sword because he fails to understand history. As to that fellow, Tenea . . .
PAPUC: I've smelt a rat for years. Had I not been secretly spying on him we would all be in the clutches of Dan's executioners by now.
VLAD: I suspected him because I . . . [*After a pause*] Did you say Dan wants to speak with me?
PAPUC: I presumed so – the proud, wild Dan.
VLAD: We'll enjoy discussing things with him over the service.
PAPUC: What service?
VLAD: His burial service. After all, if he's a Christian we shan't bury him like a heathen. But first he'll have to dig his own

grave. As deep as possible, wide and comfortable. We'll bury him – alive!

PAPUC: [*Looks at him to see whether he is joking*] Good God! [*Papuc then exits*]

Scene 4

Enter STELNIŢA *dressed for battle, accompanied by Branişte and Lungu.*

STELNIŢA: [*Panting*] It's over, they're done for!

VLAD: Who are done for?

STELNIŢA: The Turks. They've crossed the Danube. We'll beat them hollow. [*Seriously*] There's not enough room for them all in our traps. My soldiers are ready though. Branişte has run away from boyar Dan's estate so he can fight in Your Highness's army.

BRANIŞTE: Of course I ran away! Ran all the way here!

VLAD: At last! The battle I've been waiting for all my life. The enemies inside are now outside and those on the outside are inside. God, it was lucky the weather was on our side!

Enter a group of Captains, all prepared for battle

ACT
FOUR

Evening

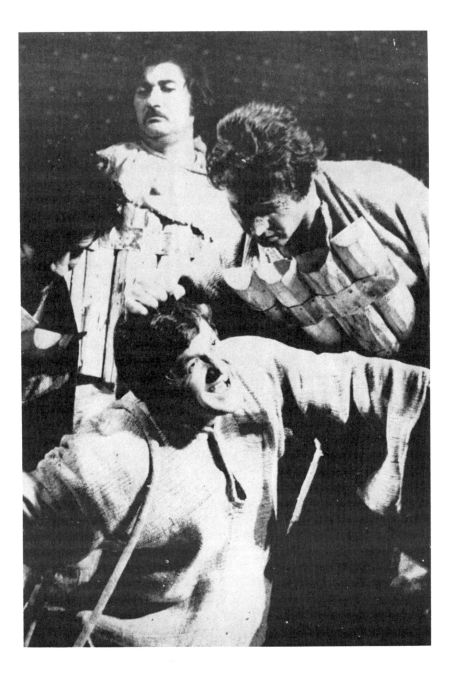

Scene 1

Ten years later. A cell in a tower of the prison at Buda. Semi-darkness. One can just see the thick walls with many rat holes, like many blind windows. One of Vlad's standards is stuck somewhere in the wall. The canvas has rotted with age and damp. His spear looks like a rusty stake.

VLAD: [*Sitting cross-legged in the middle of the cell, sewing something. He stops working and takes a long look around*] Good God! It's ten years since we started doing needlwork!

PAPUC: [*Sadly*] Sewing rags together instead of human destinies!

VLAD: It'll be ten years on the Feast of the Assumption. And when is Saint Expectation day?

PAPUC: Perhaps they'll set us free before then.

VLAD: [*Stands up. He is thin, his face is drawn and his eyes glitter. He stretches himself, cracking all his bones, and then yawns*] We ended up here because of the Turks and here we sit cross-legged like them. [*Shaking the rags he is sewing – a Turkish costume, shalwars and vest*] I've made a Turkish costume. Do you like the vest?

PAPUC: I'd have thought you could've sewn better than that after all these years [*Laughs*] The needle's small, not like a stake.

VLAD: [*Annoyed*] I hadn't much thread or material. The rats brought me these bits. They didn't like to come – empty-handed. [*Admiring the shalwars*] You can't deny I've made a good job of the shalwars. They're really good. [*Puts the rags aside*] Everyone should learn a trade. And learn it from a child. Otherwise . . .

PAPUC: . . . he learns it when he's no longer . . . great.

VLAD: [*Proudly*] They took my throne from me, but I've still been a prince all these years. I fought, I defended the country against rats, against the enemy inside . . . [*Stares at a hole*] who keep in touch with the enemy outside the country, under your very nose. We've got to stop these comings and goings, whatever it costs. It spells anarchy, Captain!

89

PAPUC: Your Highness [*Emerging from a cranny pulling his chains with him*]

VLAD: My breastplate!

PAPUC: It's gone rusty.

VLAD: [*Puts it on*] . . . and it's grown too loose for me.

PAPUC: I don't know why one gets thinner in jail.

VLAD: [*Looking about him*] Are all your soldiers at their posts?

PAPUC: [*Listlessly*] Possibly.

VLAD: I'll get my own back in the end. You'll end up on a stake like everyone else!

PAPUC: I've spent all my life among spikes and spines just like hedgehogs.

VLAD: Give me your sword. [*Papuc fetches a wooden sword*] A fine sword! Do you know something?

PAPUC: No, what?

VLAD: We never had good weapons or enough of them and yet we had to fight. You know your position! [*Papuc moves away a few steps, kneels and puts his ear to the ground. He listens.*]

PAPUC: I can hear rumbling.

VLAD: Let them rumble! They think we don't know of their plans. Quick, go and cover the window. [*Papuc crawls over to a small window, as big as a fist, and covers it with a rag*] Darkness makes them less cautious. [*Vlad also kneels. There is a tense moment*] Why can't I catch mice when I trim my moustache? [*Slight noise followed by a roar*] Hurray! Forward! [*Starts to run about the cell*] That's it, you villain. Now I've got you! [*Walks downstage holding a writhing rat by its tail*] This is Dan [*Pointing to a corner*] Tenea is over there. No, it's the pasha. First I named them and after gave them a nickname.

PAPUC: Shall we hoist the victory flag?

VLAD: As high as you can! [*Papuc takes hold of the flag, a rag, and hoists it up a little higher*] You scum, have you never heard of me? Vlad, the Prince of Wallachia who for ten years has been fighting rats in the prison of Matthew Corvin in Buda? That kinsman of ours – that great fool!

PAPUC: Not so loud! [*Pointing to the walls*] They have ears!

VLAD: So have I, and for years I've heard only your whimpering and the squeaking of the enemy. [*Goes in one corner of the cell. One can discern in the darkness a row of small stakes where rats are impaled*] At last I've learned just how many kinds of rats live in this world: yellow, black, orange, indigo and violet. Are there striped rats as well? Those who live in prisons should be striped, if it's only out of a sense of solidarity with the inmates – those poor wretches who keep them alive. This one isn't striped. So he's not sorry for us and deserves his fate! [*He is about to impale him, then changes his mind*] I've changed my mind. [*Pondering*] So far I've done it because I'm shy of the other side of my nature, so as not to show my lyrical temperament. That's why I've sharpened my sense of sight, hearing and touch on living creatures.

PAPUC: [*Insisting*] And the second?

VLAD: Nothing.

PAPUC: At least one.

VLAD: Not one.

PAPUC: They wanted to tear out your throat and would have done if I hadn't come to the rescue – just in time. Only yesterday too, while you were asleep. Go on, this one at least.

VLAD: I'm fasting. And then I'll wash my hands.

Light on stage

PAPUC: [*His hands are empty*] I let it go!

VLAD: Let it go! I'll let mine go too.

PAPUC: Have you turned monk overnight, and I didn't know?

VLAD: [*Sadly*] I was too cruel. They put the blame on me for everything. That's how legends are born. They say I hacked three hundred boyars to pieces. There weren't three hundred in the whole of Wallachia and the other Romanian lands put together. They say I made three hundred people boyars after I'd given their kaftans, I killed him off because they were no good. Just you show me one good one and I'll swallow him up. No, my fault's somewhere else. I had no time to make friends with the people once I'd started to do all the good I was planning. It's true that practically no one offered to help. Europe left me to face the Turks alone. And all alone here . . .

PAPUC: There are bound to be things that aren't true, but then you can bear it all!

VLAD: How can one justify crime? Even to kill rats is like killing people.

PAPUC: What does the life of an individual matter compared to that of the homeland.

VLAD: Sometimes I sit and think about some of those boyars. I could have pardoned some of them. And it would have served the country.

PAPUC: They say the word LONGING is untranslatable.

VLAD: It is in Turkish.

PAPUC: In Turkish? What do the Turks say then?

VLAD: Bugger off! [*Papuc laughs*] I was a hostage in Constantinople and I wrote to my father that I missed my country. He answered me in Turkish, SIKTIR BRE! Bugger off!

PAPUC: Yes, but I think the Turkish words don't have the exact meaning of the Romanian.

VLAD: Sometimes they do and sometimes they don't. [*Sighing*] Now I miss my country again. Badly. Let's . . . go home.

PAPUC: [*After a while*] Is it possible that all your energies have not borne fruit? It wouldn't surprise me.

VLAD: Is that what's eating you? I'm sure the stakes have long since rotted, the crows are fatter, the corpses ripe and on the point of falling from the tree. A good bone often falls into the mouth of a bad dog. Now who could that bad dog be, eh? Radu? Laoita? For Dan . . .

PAPUC: Whatever we all did. It couldn't have been wrong, for we did it out of patriotism. If we hadn't acted, the country would have been a Turkish colony by now. An iron discipline was just what they needed.

VLAD: My breastplate's gone rusty since that idiot, Matthew . . .

PAPUC: He'll order them to release me from prison and then you'll be left alone. You know I came of my own free will; I had to beg him on bended knee to let me keep you company, so you'd have someone to quarrel with . . . to while away the time . . . and make plans for the future with.

VLAD: We've always been good at making plans.

PAPUC: So we'd know what to do if you were ever on the throne of Wallachia again.

VLAD: You stuck to me like a burr . . . to spy on me.

PAPUC: I let them beat me, so they wouldn't beat you.

VLAD: They put you in here so you'd know what I was thinking, so you'd inform on me. Or were you sorry to have sold me out? Who did forget that letter to the Sultan?

PAPUC: If only I knew! In any case it was probably some German from Braşov who wanted to avenge himself.

VLAD: And why was the king of Hungary such a fool as to think I'd betray him? That was some lie!

PAPUC: I don't know. Perhaps it suited him. He was always afraid of Your Highness.

VLAD: [*Looking at the rats*] Before we killed them we should have found out what was going on outside.

PAPUC: They'd only have complained of the lack of holes.

VLAD: Well, at least we've got one. [*Looking at the stakes*] There are lots of stakes but not enough to terrorize them. The moment you blow out the candle, they pounce on you. They're clever enough to even get through a buttonhole. You have to sleep with your armour on 'cos they'll gnaw through anything.

PAPUC: At your command!

VLAD: When are these invasions going to stop?

PAPUC: I think that . . .

VLAD: Don't say that . . . [*Losing his temper*]

PAPUC: There are too many holes. No sooner do you watch one than they come up on the other side. The moment you turn your back they bite your bottom. The whole world's teeming with them.

VLAD: Will I never be able to exterminate them all?

PAPUC: Look out! [*Runs to catch a rat*]

VLAD: You missed it! [*He flies at him*] Never speak to me during a battle. We're talking while the enemy charges! [*Raises a threatening fist in the direction of the holes*] I'll show you! [*To Papuc*] I'll not fast any more. This is what we'll do; dig a ditch and fill it with water. Bring water!

PAPUC: Our drinking water! It's the ration for the week. [*Hands him a bucket full of water. Vlad pours it into the ditch.*]

VLAD: Never mind! [*Splashes are heard*] Listen! Do you hear?

PAPUC: They swim like devils.

VLAD: [*Catching one*] We'll fish for soaking devils. [*Impales it. After a pause*] Do you think I'm mad?

PAPUC: No.

VLAD: Then what do you think?

PAPUC: I think . . . I've stopped thinking.

VLAD: Why? Have you turned stupid? [*Papuc is silent*] So, you came to prison just for my sake, eh?

PAPUC: I've always supported Your Highness.

VLAD: You've been a faithful servant.

PAPUC: I was.

VLAD: You're proud of that fact. [*A pause*] Do you think we'll ever get out of here in one piece?

PAPUC: Of course we will, even if it means squeezing out through one of these holes. Ten years have gone by and we've hardly noticed it.

VLAD: You counted the years. Good for you! When we get out of here we'll know the exact date. What day of the week is it now?

PAPUC: I think it's Thursday.

VLAD: Thursday?

PAPUC: Or Wednesday.

VLAD: [*Afraid*] Wednesday?

PAPUC: Or Saturday.

VLAD: [*Laughing*] To hell with the days of the week. They're all the same. [*A pause*] Do you think we'll be fighting against the Turks again?

PAPUC: Who else?

VLAD: Someone else may have beaten them by now and we'll be able to mount the throne . . . and tell stories.

PAPUC: Europe is governed by milksops. They're all milksops. We rot in here because of idiots. Do you know what we should do when we get out of here? We should dress the whole army in Turkish uniforms . . . and conquer the lot of them.

VLAD: [*Laughing*] It would do them a world of good.

PAPUC: [*Thoughtfully*] Still. I think our plan is marvellous.

VLAD: Do you? Look! [*Points to the ground to show the place where he has scratched something with a stick*] Here's the map of Wallachia.

PAPUC: The rats have gnawed away at it, Your Highness.

VLAD: We'll snatch it from their jaws. Never before have we had so much time to prepare a battle. Too much perhaps. Will we ever be able to fight?

PAPUC: For the time being . . . [*Points to a hole*] here, at the gates of the East.

VLAD: [*An idea flashes through his mind*] Not bad! That gives me an idea! What if . . . Do you know what? Look this way. It's a bit narrow . . . but probably gets wider further on. Rats don't like to be cramped up either. There's only room for my hand, but we can make it wider. Come over here, we've work to do. [*Darkness; after a brief pause*] I think it's ready now.

PAPUC: It's only the rats who'll benefit. Now they can rush in at us two at a time.

VLAD: Rats?

PAPUC: Who else? They'll be grateful to us if they've been cramped up for so long.

VLAD: They won't rush in because it'll be us who'll pounce on them. Put your head in the hole.

PAPUC: [*Afraid*] Me?

VLAD: Put in your head and say what you can see. [*Papuc hesitates*] Stop hesitating. We've no time to lose. [*Papuc obeys. Puts out his head, terrified*] The Turks are out there. The whole country is waiting for us. For the great battle. There's only this filthy prison between us and them. [*Laughs grimly*]

PAPUC: My God, what a mess. For so many years! [*A brief pause*]

VLAD: [*Paces the cell impatiently, then stops to take a long look, as though looking out of a window*] The weather's changing.

PAPUC: It never changes.

VLAD: Look, the poplars are bending.

PAPUC: Your Highness, you're looking through the wall. That's not the window!

VLAD: Then it's a door. There are times when one can see through a door.

PAPUC: If only there were such a door . . . still, there is a door somewhere, but I can't remember where. It's been shut for so long.

VLAD: Each time I look through the window a great wave of sadness comes over me. Sadness and disgust . . . and a longing for my country . . . [*Sighs*]

PAPUC: Waves and waves, that's probably how the sea was born.

VLAD: That's why it's so bitter.

PAPUC: So black.

VLAD: So far away.

Scene 2

The door opens: the painter enters carrying a big painting in a frame. He hangs it somewhere on the wall. Takes a look at it, then tries hanging it somewhere else.

PAINTER: [*Looking at the painting*] It will need more light.

VLAD: [*To Papuc. Reproachfully*] You see? Remember what I told you? We need more light [*Goes to take a closer look at the painting*] Who's that ghost?

PAINTER: [*Bowing*] Your Highness. [*Bowing to the painting*] It is you, my Lord.

VLAD: [*Taking him in his arms*] How did you get here, master painter?

PAINTER: [*Smiling*] Easy. Art can penetrate even into prison.

VLAD: Am I an artist then?

PAINTER: Yes, in your own way! Perhaps even a genius. [*Taking him by the hand and leading him to the painting*] Are you aware what this hallucinating countenance reveals? Pure genius.

VLAD: [*Calmly examining the painting*] Who is he? The new reigning prince? You've joined this one too, eh? Well, who is he?

PAINTER: Who are you talking about?

VLAD: The fellow in the painting.

PAINTER: [*Surprised*] You're joking! [*Annoyed*] Don't you remember sitting for me on your throne?

VLAD: What throne?

PAINTER: You always allowed me in your presence so that I might catch . . .

VLAD: . . . me red-handed!

PAINTER: . . . your expressions. I was also on the battlefield. I searched your soul. Then I watched you as you acted in that dreadful event. I lost my hand there, painting your portrait, following you about, palette in hand, and I managed to enter the Turkish camp. [*Proudly*] This is my best piece. [*Sadly*] The Dictionary . . . I had started on a dictionary, a hobby of mine. Radu's soldiers took it from me – during a search. Lost. The gypsies stole it and made paper cornets for pumpkin seeds out of it. The seeds they sell at fairs. Then another search – they searched every nook and cranny of my home. Under the fireplace – the floorboards, in order to find odd pages. I fussed over every word I wrote – native, Latin, Turkish.

VLAD: In Wallachia, nothing's safe even in your own home. Is that what we fought for, Papuc?

PAINTER: I did complain about it to Tenea, Radu's councillor: 'I should like you to establish my status as citizen of Europe, once and for all. I don't want always to be at the mercy of your mercenaries.' I should have left for Italy on the spot, in protest, only Domnica refused to go. 'No, not Italy. Our children must learn Romanian . . . first.' How could they learn it if they weren't allowed to use Romanian words? So, first my wife and then my dictionary kept me here.

PAPUC: And the mercenaries!

PAINTER: Yes, and the mercenaries. I almost forgot them. [*Looking at the portrait*] My finest work!

VLAD: Perhaps it is. But . . . who's that? [*In a fit of anger*] That

96

ghost! [*In a softer voice*] Well, who can tell? Perhaps I am a ghost now. [*Examining the painting*] Can this forehead frown and crush thoughts between its wrinkles as if they were snakes hiding in nooks and crannies? Can it frown when the earth quakes?

PAINTER: It can indeed.

VLAD: That is the moustache of a man who has time to look at himself in the mirror. In a full-length mirror. I for one had one painful fragment of a country to stare to. I had no time to trim a moustache in the mirror. Only time to see who else was coming. And they were all coming. To see what was to be done. And there was so much to be done. [*In a faint voice*] Why do you bring me such gaudy pictures?

PAINTER: [*Sadly*] I've brought you news too.

VLAD: [*Startled*] Stop! Don't say any more!

PAPUC: [*Curious, he approaches the painter*] Well, what is the news?

VLAD: I'll tell you what the news is: they've taken away our right to stay even in prison. [*Pointing to the painting*] and we shall be sent to kingdom come. Everything is for the best.

PAINTER: You'll be the reigning prince again. King Matthew is now convinced of your innocence. Stephen, prince of Moldavia, will give you every support in regaining your throne.

VLAD: Stephen . . . him again . . . I helped him mount his throne and yet he helped me to lose mine.

PAINTER: Stephen is your friend . . . A good man! He's done a lot of harm to the heathens. He would have courage to do more should Your Highness reign in Wallachia. He has been interceding with Prince Matthew in order to set you free. I painted his portrait on condition that he allowed me to see you and be the first to break the news to you.

PAPUC: [*Leaping with joy as high as his chains allow*] Justice will out! Justice will out!

VLAD: Yes, but it isn't out yet. Wait and see the finale.

PAPUC: Truth and justice have always triumphed.

VLAD: [*Sarcastically*] Of course they have . . . [*Tapping the painter on the shoulder*] I'm sorry I can't cry. I'd like to, but I can't. [*In a different tone of voice*] I'm glad to see you, friend. We'll wait and see. We'll die . . . if we're meant to die, or we'll live . . . if we're meant to live. Come let's talk it over.

PAINTER: [*Thoughtfully; he takes down the painting and is about to go*] I'm a failure. And when I think of the plans, the sleepless nights . . . I had my doubts and now they've been proved true. I wanted to portray the mystery behind Your Highness's personality. [*In a different tone of voice*] Had you heard that books about Dracula the Terrible are being circulated all over Europe? The text is interesting – if rather fantastic, but the illustrations are dreadful. [*Sighing*] I've often seen Dracula, but it appears it was all in vain . . . and I'm too old to begin all over again.

VLAD: I was Dracula and it seems it was all in vain. In a way we're even now. Give me that frame! [*Takes the painting from the frame and steps into the frame to replace the canvas*] What do you think of this portrait? [*The painter remains silent*]

PAPUC: [*Listlessly*] Leave the frame, Sir. The country's waiting for you.

VLAD: And the country within the frame . . . a Turkish frame . . . They must take me as I am, if not, I'll stay here. Meanwhile, please master painter, hang me on the wall. [*Roars with laughter*]

The painter takes his painting and is about to go.

PAINTER: My wife, Domnica, sends you her best wishes.

VLAD: Your wife?

PAINTER: That's what I ended up with . . . minus a hand.

VLAD: You've still got the other one. Any children?

PAINTER: Yes. Vlad and Domnica. It was her wish that we gave them Romanian names.

VLAD: Well, take good care of Vlad! [*Bursts out laughing again. The Painter steals away*]

Scene 3

VLAD: [*After a pause, he leaves the frame and goes over to Papuc*] Did you hear that? Did you see? Or was it just my imagination? [*After a pause*] Listen Papuc. Do you think there's any chance of us mounting the throne again?

PAPUC: Yes, of course there is!

VLAD: Are you sure?

PAPUC: Well I think so.

VLAD: And who shall we fight against?

PAPUC: [*Laughing*] What a question! The Turks of course. We're used to it by now. No point in changing the enemy.

VLAD: With the Turks, eh? . . . I don't really feel mad at them any more. That's why I'm afraid. It's weakened me . . . this prison . . . and the time I've been shut up here. Papuc!

PAPUC: Sire!

VLAD: Do you love your country?

PAPUC: [*Afraid*] What sort of question is that? If I hadn't loved it . . .

VLAD: [*Thoughtfully*] So . . . you say you are fond of it.

PAPUC: It's my be-all-and-end-all.

VLAD: Your be-all-and-end-all, eh?

PAPUC: That's why I followed Your Highness here . . . faithfully.

VLAD: If someone else had been on the throne you might have come off a bit better.

PAPUC: Well, I know very well how things were. [*Dreamily*] The day you're back on the throne, we'll start from the beginning again . . . How happy the people will be!

VLAD: Do you think they'll have forgotten me?

PAPUC: Who? Your Highness? [*Laughing*] They were only just learning to fear you.

VLAD: I don't want to make them afraid. I was cruel, but I suffered for it too. Times were bad. Times when there could be no pity, no pardon. Minica was right when he wanted to get away, to live in the past or in the future . . . anything but the present. As for me, I was the reigning prince. I had to defend my country against the Turks, and the rats. Pity and pardon are tasty meals I have no right to enjoy. My diet was different and that's why my kidneys hurt so much. [*Walks about the cell tortured by thoughts*] Listen Papuc . . . I was just thinking . . .

PAPUC: Thinking?

VLAD: I can't remember what a Turk looks like. I'm afraid I'll leave this place dressed up for battle with coat of mail, sword, and so on, and instead of attacking them I'll start chasing rats.

PAPUC: [*Laughing*] That's a good one . . . Now I understand! You've made that Turkish costume so that you . . .

VLAD: [*Picks up the costume*] Here are the clothes, but where's the Turk. I know! Put them on.

99

PAPUC: What, you want me to play the Turk? I won't do it. I'll get dirty.

VLAD: Come on, you said you were patriotic.

PAPUC: No.

VLAD: Don't be so stubborn. [*Laughs*]

PAPUC: [*Putting on the costume*] This reminds me of when I was looking for Mahommed's tent, sword at the ready. We only missed it because the moon went behind a cloud!

VLAD: [*Looking him up and down*] You're a real Turk, Papuc!

PAPUC: Brave! [*A frightened rat scurries between their feet*]

VLAD: Get it! [*They both dive to the ground to catch it*] It's gone.

PAPUC: The country's a long way off, but the enemy is near at hand.

VLAD: Where is it? [*Papuc points to a hold in the wall*] Put your head in and see where it's gone to. It must be caught. If we fail to get that one, we'll never regain the throne. That's what I'm beginning to think . . . Oh, listen to me telling my own fortune now!

PAPUC: [*Putting his head in the hole*] I can't hear a thing.

VLAD: Take a really good look [*Seizes the spear on which the ragged flag if flying and moves close to Papuc*] Villain! You shopped me!

PAPUC: [*His head still in the hole*] I can't hear a word you're saying!

VLAD: If you hadn't been a spy they'd never have let you stay with me. They sent you to spy on me.

PAPUC: Speak up. I can't hear you. Oh the rats are making for my throat . . .

VLAD: Get them then! we're sure to get the better of them! [*Thrusts the spear into his body as hard as he can . . . Papuc roars with pain . . . Rats are heard squeaking. After a moment's silence . . .*] One Turk less. The one man who really loved me. Even more than a mother. But these are terrible times and who better than your own kin to help you sharpen your anger? I've still got strength in my arm and the years spent in prison haven't distorted my sense of justice. Even if I have to cut off my own limbs to prove it. The country still needs this iron hand.

The door opens. Light rushes in

100

ACT
FIVE

Morning

Scene 1

In the forest. The same setting as for Act One.

ROMANIAN: The strangest thing, friend, is that we're not dead yet. Time's passed and a lot's been going on around us. There've been two or three reigning princes.

TURK: Ah, but are the changes for the better?

ROMANIAN: Of course, 'cos things are no different from when we started.

TURK: No different?

ROMANIAN: No, no different . . . Vlad. He's on the throne for the second time and I'll bet he'll be surprised to find we didn't die at least once during his first reign. We're lagging behind, can't keep up any more. We're old now.

TURK: Perhaps because we're in such a sorry state, we only imagined time passing. Perhaps only a moment passed . . . a brief moment.

ROMANIAN: Not long ago, a raven passed and dropped a ripe mulberry on your lips. Is it a good crop this year?

TURK: The black ones are ready. Those that stain. The mulberries are ready, but the others aren't. The birds feed us with God's gifts.

ROMANIAN: The high and mighty are always the best off. It's obviously painful but I've grown used to it.

TURK: An age-old pain. It was painful in my mother's womb, but I got used to it, didn't I?

ROMANIAN: Almost a death. A natural death . . . Just a way of life. Man can never be severed from matter, on the contrary he penetrates into it.

TURK: Man is matter and nature is – history.

ROMANIAN: Romanians and history are like brothers.

TURK: Rain washes us, even if it's only a drop. Rain water has soda in it.

ROMANIAN: Then don't taste it!

TURK: Why taste?

ROMANIAN: [*Sighing*] And so time went by . . .

TURK: We've watched time pass from here, from on high . . .

ROMANIAN: God, the things we've seen! A lot's changed . . . for the better, as I was saying . . . other princes came, took a look at us and never lifted a finger to help. They just looked. At least Vlad talked to the people, with the oppressed.

TURK: He didn't say anything last night.

ROMANIAN: When?

TURK: Around midnight; he came here, ate something under the stakes and didn't say a thing. You were asleep – perhaps he didn't want to disturb you. He was lost in thought. Notching a few words on that middle stake. Can you see what he wrote? Any news?

ROMANIAN: Yes [*Reads*] Vlad.

TURK: So he's taken control of the country.

TURK: All the reigning princes who came after him did nothing but move everyone on a two-pronged stake.

TURK: That's all part of the policy too.

ROMANIAN: They must have thought we were blood brothers, coming from the same stable, as the saying goes . . . Then another prince came and said there wasn't enough room for everyone on the same stake. We'd be far better off scattered around on our own stakes. That's also part of the policy.

TURK: So, it's all similar to the history of Vlad's reign. He defeated Mohammed but lost his throne soon afterwards. Yet Mohammed didn't fare any better and now Vlad's back all ready to make a fresh start and with renewed energy.

ROMANIAN: Mere guesswork. You lived among strangers who've probably influenced you. You bring grist to their mill without realizing it . . .

TURK: Well, let's not quarrel when we're near the end now.

ROMANIAN: You and your theories! You wear me down.

TURK: All right, I'll change my way of thinking. Everything's going to finish fine. At least as far as we're concerned.

ROMANIAN: And even if your theories were right, such ambiguity only serves some lofty purpose of which, at this moment, we are completely unaware. It's a matter of survival.

TURK: Look, I for one came here to be buried, at least in the soil of my own country. They've killed me . . . that's a fact, but instead of burying me, I'm left here stuck in the air.

ROMANIAN: An open ending, perhaps . . . [*A Pause*] What surprises me is that in the beginning everything was going fine and now we're always ready to quarrel. And recently it happens more often.

TURK: We may have had some disagreements. That's natural. Just think, even hills can be split apart by seeping water. Anyway, several years have passed.

ROMANIAN: Do you think water has seeped into our friendship? Unfortunately, things aren't the same. I've always told you the truth but you've been telling me a pack of lies.

TURK: Me? When?

ROMANIAN: You've tried to make concessions, more and more important ones. So we were bound to fall out! You got round the prince!

TURK: [*Amazed*] Why should I want to do that? I only spoke my thoughts . . . and I'm pleased to say that on many issues we thought alike.

ROMANIAN: Don't say that! It's you who made your opinions coincide.

TURK: If only you could overcome your own personal agonies and look at things impartially, you'd be able to see that he did do a lot of good. I know he impaled us, but he's also done a lot of good things in his time. That's what you told me.

ROMANIAN: Me?

TURK: In your sleep.

ROMANIAN: No!

TURK: The moment your eyes are closed you start raving with pain and then sing his praises. You actually rave in dithyrambs.

ROMANIAN: It's true that at times I can quite like him, but some of his actions I've judged very severely and told him so, to his face!

TURK: If you hadn't, you wouldn't be here like this today! [*A pause*] To prove I'm still your friend I'll let you into a secret. Put your ear a little closer. [*The Romanian pretends to do so*] You must realize that I'm not . . . the same man I used to be.

ROMANIAN: Not the same?

TURK: I'm not as I was at first. A long time's passed since then and in the meantime they've put another Turk in my place.

ROMANIAN: You're scaring me. That is . . . wait a bit . . . Didn't you have a little mole on the left cheek? . . . and now it's a war.

ROMANIAN: Now, listen to me. I know what I'm on about: I died about ten years ago and they put someone else in my place.

ROMANIAN: How come I didn't notice?

TURK: Well, I'm just like the other one. And let me tell you something else. Turn the other ear. [*The Romanian pretends to do so*] You're not the same man either!

ROMANIAN: Not the same?

TURK: No!

ROMANIAN: Another, just like the first?

TURK: Yes!

ROMANIAN: Damn those wretches! Why didn't they say they'd changed us?

TURK: Well they did say there'd be great changes. We should have got that into our thick skulls.

ROMANIAN: So maybe Vlad has changed too.

TURK: There were others in his stead, and now he's just the same. His second reign . . .

ROMANIAN: But he's as good as new . . . I'd like to feel my body but there's nothing I can use to touch it with . . . and besides, there's nothing I can . . .

TURK: The hand only pretends to exist. The body pretends to exist and feel the hand that touches it.

ROMANIAN: If only we'd been able to touch ourselves in time we'd have realized. And why replace us with someone identical?

TURK: It's a matter of talking to each other. They realized we were getting along fine . . . so to speak.

ROMANIAN: Well, I think we're the same ones who were impaled, because everything fits together.

TURK: You're as stubborn as a Turk who refuses to understand.

ROMANIAN: Well, I came here from Turkey. Wasn't I taken away from my mother's breast and sold as tribute?

TURK: [*Laughing*] Don't you see? You've started mixing both of us up. That was me . . . you were . . . the other one. I kept telling you the way things were in Turkey and now you're convinced you're me.

ROMANIAN: What a mess! Have we gone off our heads now?

TURK: [*Sadly*] That's what happens when you vegetate. Now let me tell you the good news. We're no longer the ones who replaced the first ones who were impaled . . . it's too long ago for that . . . We're different again.

ROMANIAN: [*Annoyed*] Oh, to hell with the whole blasted lot of them! It's always the same. Some want to run away, others want to come up here. Why is everyone so eager to replace us? We're not princes on a throne!

TURK: It's not a throne, but still . . .

ROMANIAN: [*Reckoning up*] This is the third generation.

TURK: The third stinking generation. Well, it just happens that . . .

ROMANIAN: We didn't come off too badly. The fowls of the air fed us with what little they had.

TURK: The rain washed us clean.

ROMANIAN: The wind brought us news . . . that got worse and worse.

TURK: Nonsense! The north wind blew the news into our ears; in one ear and out at the other.

ROMANIAN: Just like now.

TURK: What about now?

ROMANIAN: This . . . our life.

TURK: Our death. We've shaken and trembled with cold and died from thirst.

ROMANIAN: We've wanted so badly to hear good news. But instead we've only heard the wind sighing.

TURK: How well you can play a tune by just using a green leaf. In autumn, whenever a leaf fell on your lips, you played a tune.

ROMANIAN: [*Sighing*] I used a yellow leaf.
Green leaf
Of yellow sheaf.

TURK: Yes, that's right, but what about me who could only play on fish scales?

ROMANIAN: [*After a pause*] What surprises me is that he notched the year of his death on the stake.

TURK: What year?

ROMANIAN: The year of his death.

TURK: Who?

ROMANIAN: Him.

TURK: Oh I can see it! [*Spelling it out*] VLAD 1429–1476. Is that his own writing?

ROMANIAN: Yes. Last night while you were asleep he notched it with his pocket knife.

TURK: Perhaps he feels it's going to be a bad year.

ROMANIAN: The years he spent in prison weigh heavily on his mind. it seems that in the two months he's been back on the throne everything's gone from bad to worse. Rumour has it that

107

he said he'd have been better off back in prison. He's no
friends.

TURK: What about us?

ROMANIAN: Those who were close to him were butchered while he
was away. There were two left but he killed them off without a
second thought. The Turkish army is scattered throughout the
forest.

TURK: One can hear them moaning. It was a hard battle.

ROMANIAN: The prince can't muster his troups anymore . . . not
at any price. I reckon that some of his boyars have already
elected another prince in his place.

TURK: So we've come to witness troubled times.

ROMANIAN: When you're stuck here like we are, you could do with
more movement about you, more agitation and more activity.
Just think of the agitation in his heart. All that activity!

TURK: Quite!

ROMANIAN: Here he comes!

TURK: Now don't be rude to him.

ROMANIAN: I'm afraid he's wounded and wants to ask our advice
about how it feels when it hurts.

TURK: Enter VLAD. *He is pale and bleeding*

Scene 2

VLAD: A single brick doesn't have an echo, but put it in a vault and
it resounds loud enough. Oh, those echoes! I've always thought
of that vault. Bricks have never understood me. [*Walks slowly
towards the middle stake*]. I thought I'd never get here. [*Touching
his wounds under his ribs*] A Turkish arrow hit me. And then,
soon afterwards, one of ours. I could tell the difference by the
poison. The poison in our arrows and the poison in theirs has
now met in my body. Turks and Romanians. I've never been
able to avoid this symmetry. Who was the coward? Treason.
Everything was plotted years ago. Perhaps they thought me
dead. Still, that's not the sort of death we want and for which we
wasted so much material. [*Shades his eyes with his hands and
measures the stake*] I've left you naked like a wanton far too long.
[*Tries to laugh*] Ha! [*A little more cheerfully*] Look at me, passing

judgement on myself! I've dispensed justice in this country in great detail. Only one remained unpunished. Let's take advantage of this little respite to mete out fair justice according to the laws of our ancestors. [*Kneeling and in a slightly tremulous voice*] Name? Vladislav. Profession? Reigning prince. Country? Wallachia. [*A brief pause*] God willed that you should be the head of the people and have power enough to fill both heaven and hell with the guilty and the innocent. I have filled both heaven and hell. For the hell, we forgive you. God's wrath strikes as lightning upon those who do wrong. But there is great distress and much grief in heaven. You will shed tears of blood for it. I've always paid on the nail, sometimes more than was necessary. There are floods made from tears in heaven. So much so that there is no more room there. We have to press and push our way in. You will never be forgiven because the stake you prepared for Mohammed, the moment he defiled your country, stands empty. Mohammed's been and gone, alive. I'm still reigning prince over one subject. You thought that once you put the fear of death into your own subjects that the enemy would also be afraid. Your people went mad through fear but the enemy has returned. I wanted my people to be strong and upright [*Tries to get up*] Sit down. We haven't finished yet. Why do you speak Turkish? [*Laughing*] That's no fault of mine. Why should I get the blame for it? I was sent there as hostage and forced to learn it. I could have learnt Tartar too. Then why did you punish this man – a Romanian – [*Pointing to the Turk*] who is rotting here in his Turkish clothes. Why did you punish him for returning home? My men were overhasty in their judgement. Who is responsible for your men? Only one. What did you do while in prison in Buda for ten whole years? [*Laughs*] What could I have done? What anyone does in a prison. Stayed there in the dark. You left your country. I was betrayed. You shouldn't have let yourself be caught and give them an opportunity to defile a prince whom God had ordained to sit on the throne. It won't happen again. You'll receive your punishment now. The first . . . What are you waiting for? It's there in front of you. The stake. [*Looks at the stake terrified*] Mercy! [*Kisses his right hand*] Forgiveness! You ask forgiveness. As if you had ever listened to that voice! A moment of weakness. It's only human. I swear, I'm innocent and that everything I did was for the good of the country. Still, I do deserve to be punished. [*Rises and starts to climb to the stake*] Oh, if only I had strength left to reach the top! It would be like regaining my throne a third time. [*Slips down*] How slippery the road to greatness! [*Looks about him*] The horizon's getting wider and wider, as if on purpose. [*Sighing*] And for the first time I feel calm and quiet. I feel my thoughts striking against the edge of . . . of what? Mine . . . the border of the country perhaps or the edge of the world. I've done my best. Yet I'm still guilty. I'm to blame because I existed. And more particularly because I was what I was. Maybe the future will understand me. [*Laughs*] Why future if the present's so great? Look at that wide horizon! [*Climbs*] This time the battle's really lost. [*From the forest comes the sound of battle*] And they're looking for me, to catch me alive! I'm coming . . . [*To his two neighbours*] Hey! Good day to you. How are you both? You're looking well. It's as if time hadn't touched you.

ROMANIAN: [*In a faint voice*] No, it's not the years that have passed by, but that bloody carrion, time.

VLAD: [*No longer hearing very well*] What? I can't hear any longer. I stopped hearing these wretches years ago, though they seem to keep moving their lips as if trying to tell me something. They keep on talking, but words no longer reach me. Let's get closer . . . [*Climbs again*] Closer . . . They ought not to be left alone when they're in trouble. Nor I left alone without them. It's your turn now lads to defend me . . . I've moved the council to here! [*He's almost reached the top*] I've started feeling the edge of destiny with the palm of my hand. When I feel it with my heart they'll know whether or not I really had a heart of stone. I'm quite keen to find out myself. [*To the Romanian*] Good morning, Romanian! Good morning, Turk! Good night, world! [*To the horizon*] Good night, motley world! Morning, noon and night. You've suffered only for yourselves, I've suffered for everyone. In vain? Who knows! For the time being, night's closing in . . . we must bid ourselves a 'goodnight' [*Solemnly*] Good night, Prince Vlad, riding a restless hedgehog! [*Laughs. To the two men*] Are you crying? Or is it just that the raindrops in your eyes haven't dried up yet? I've always avoided tears all my life, and still I seem fated to have had tears always about me. Tragedy! I can tell you all about that! It's less than a thousand years since the soldiers living in these parts died laughing, throwing themselves upon a bed of spears. The spears were left in the ground; they rooted, grew fast and became forests. But why don't we laugh any more? Is death such a bad thing that it keeps our jaws clamped? Is it? [*Laughs*] Ha! Ha! If they're clamped we'll open them with a stake. [*Sadly*] What a pity that just when you start to relax everything's over . . . let's climb higher. [*Climbs*] I bow respectfully to this kingdom, to the power and the glory!

CURTAIN

Other FOREST BOOKS publications by MARIN SORESCU from the
EAST EUROPEAN SERIES

LET'S TALK ABOUT THE WEATHER

Selected poetry translated by Andrea Deletant and Brenda Walker
Introduction by Jon Silkin

0 9509487 8 0   £5.95 paper

THE THIRST OF THE SALT MOUNTAIN

Three plays JONAH, THE VERGER and THE MATRIX translated
by Andrea Deletant and Brenda Walker Introduction by Marin Sorescu

0 9509487 5 6   £6.95 paper